GREEN &BLACK'S

CHOCOLATE RECIPES

The mysterious *Theobroma cacao* grows wild in the Amazon River Basin and the foothills of the Venezuelan and Colombian Andes, where it is believed the first cacao trees were first found.

GREEN &BLACK'S

CHOCOLATE RECIPES

FROM THE CACAO POD
TO MUFFINS, MOUSSES AND MOLES

Written and compiled by Caroline Jeremy
Photography by Francesca Yorke
Designed by Claire Fry

KYLE CATHIE LIMITED

'Chocolate makes otherwise normal people melt into strange states of ecstasy' *John West*

To the Maya cacao farmers
and all those cooks who have shared
their recipes over the years.

CONTENTS

FOREWORD BY JOSEPHINE FAIRLEY

When Green & Black's was launched in 1991, we cheekily declared it to be 'guilt-free' chocolate. As the world's very first organic chocolate, it gave passionate chocolate-lovers a way to indulge their tastebuds without having an environmental impact – because conventionally grown cacao is still one of the most heavily sprayed food crops in the world. Because Green & Black's was organic – just beginning, then, to be a buzzword – people were intrigued enough to buy and try it. But we know that what makes someone buy any Green & Black's treat a second time – and a hundredth time – is sheer deliciousness. Quite simply, every new Green & Black's creation has to be the best of its kind that we've ever tasted. End of story.

Gradually, though, in the last decade, most of us have begun to think much more about where our food comes from. And at Green & Black's, we like to think we've helped change the world – one bar of chocolate at a time. Because we weren't just the world's first organic chocolate. In 1993, our orange-and-spice Maya Gold Chocolate became the very first product to carry the Fairtrade Mark – the shopper's guarantee that the farmers and growers who produce our cacao get a fairer price for their crops.

This was a shopping revolution. The day of Maya Gold's launch, Green & Black's had a total of eight minutes' of news coverage on primetime TV. Because Maya Gold's debut coincided with an independent campaign for fair trade, we discovered to our astonishment that thousands of Young Methodists were actually running from town to town carrying flaming torches and button-holing supermarket managers to stock this ground-breaking Fairtrade-marked product. One supermarket buyer complained to us that he'd even been getting phone calls from vicars, badgering him to stock Maya Gold because of its ethical integrity. (Nothing to do with us, though we were secretly thrilled to have that unexpected boost to our sales drive!) But that buyer still placed an order – and today, awareness of fair trade issues means most global coffee-shop empires even offer a Fairtrade-marked *cappuccino* on their menus, while shoppers can fill shopping baskets not only with fairly traded chocolate and cocoa powder, but tea, coffee, bananas and more.

Actually, we didn't have to do anything very special to get that Fairtrade Mark: it was how we naturally did business. It was only later that we realised that we had established a blueprint for socially responsible business which many big companies are striving towards, today. Green & Black's already paid a higher price than the world price – because we offered a premium for organic beans. We gave the farmers the security of long-term contracts – because we also needed that security, at a time when organic cocoa wasn't traded anywhere on the world markets and we needed to be sure of a reliable supply. Since then, though, we've been able to see the incredible impact that fair trade has on a community.

When we first started buying cacao from the Maya Indians in Belize, children left school at eleven because their parents couldn't pay for their board during the week at the secondary school in Punta Gorda, or even afford their essential secondary school books. Now, as a result of the secure income from Green & Black's, a whole generation of children from the hillside villages where our chocolate grows is being educated to the age of eighteen; some are even attending university and at least one plans to study medicine. As Cayetano Ico, the former chairman of the co-operative of cacao farmers who produce the cacao for Maya Gold once said: 'when you buy a bar of Green & Black's, you're sending a child to school'. Shopping ethically really does change lives and communities for the better. But we've always believed: fairly traded products also have to be as yummy – or yummier – than what else is out there. Or shoppers won't buy something more than once, and the lives of Third World farmers and growers won't be transformed, after all.

People often ask how Green & Black's got its name. In fact, it was dreamed up one rainy Saturday night by me and my husband, Whole Earth Foods founder (and now Chairman of the Soil Association), Craig Sams, while searching for a name for the chocolate we planned to launch together. There was never a Mr. Green & a Mr. Black, I'm afraid: just a couple sitting in bed with a notepad and a pen, having terrific fun brainstorming. As a lifelong sweet-lover, I remembered confectionery brands from my childhood, that had stayed in my mind: Callard & Bowser, Barker & Dobson. And so Green (because it was organic) & Black's (because the chocolate was such a dark brown, it was almost black) was born. If we'd stuck to some of the names we originally batted back and forth – like 'Eco-Choc' or 'Bio-Choc' – that very same dark chocolate would simply have gathered dust on the shelves, and very few people would have discovered its tastebud-caressing deliciousness. And I don't somehow feel I'd be writing the introduction to a cookbook devoted to it.

Our other important 'first', meanwhile, was that Green & Black's was the first 70% cocoa solids chocolate available in the UK. On the Continent, chocolate *aficionados* have long enjoyed the rich, bitter intensity of really dark chocolate. Here, the 'dark' chocolate we all grew up with actually contained as little as 30% cocoa. But since Green & Black's was launched, 70% dark chocolate has become the magic figure quoted by cookery writers and superchefs whenever they publish a recipe that uses chocolate: quite simply, for the ultimate in chocolatiness, there's nothing better.

In the early days at Green & Black's, we printed a small recipe leaflet that featured recipes from leading chefs (at Launceston Place and The Groucho Club), alongside temptations from our (much-missed) friend Linda McCartney and others who'd generously shared their outrageous chocolate creations with us. We always dreamed, one day, of a Green & Black's cookbook, featuring the ultimate chocolate recipes – and here it is. Caroline Jeremy has done a marvellous job of writing this book, and collating (and testing) the many recipes we've been sent over the years, by Green & Black's lovers, and of persuading other leading cooks and chefs who are fans to reveal their chocolate recipe secrets.

We hope you enjoy making, eating and sharing them. Entirely guilt-free, naturally.

Josephine Fairley

MAGIC

The magical ingredient in chocolate comes from a pod
that grows out of the trunk of a tree.

Two recipes in one, or one very beautiful variation on a theme. The red wine jelly is a special surprise that can be served with the deep red pear clafoutis or alone as a fun end to a light meal, bringing back childhood memories of jelly and ice cream.

CLAFOUTIS WITH CHOCOLATE
AND PEARS IN RED WINE

Preparation time: 25 minutes
Cooking time: 30 minutes
Chilling time: Poach the pears about 6 hours in advance
if you plan to eat the clafoutis hot with the pear and red wine jelly
Use: 2 x tarte tatin or quiche dishes about 23cm (9in) diameter and 3–4cm (1½ in) deep
Serves: 8

6 pears, just ripe

75cl bottle red wine

juice of 1 lemon

225g (8oz) caster sugar

2 leaves gelatine

100g (3½ oz) dark chocolate,
minimum 60% cocoa solids, broken into pieces

75g (3oz) unsalted butter

110g (4oz) self-raising flour

100g (3½ oz) ground almonds

pinch of salt

2 large eggs

1 large egg yolk

175ml (6fl oz) full cream milk

Crème fraîche, to serve

Peel the pears, but leave the stalks on, then place them in a saucepan with the red wine, lemon juice and half of the caster sugar. Bring slowly to the boil, then reduce the heat to a gentle simmer and poach the pears for about 10 minutes. Turn the pears in the poaching liquid, then leave them in the liquid to cool for about 2 hours.

Reserve the liquid to make the jelly. Slice the pears in half and remove the cores carefully with a knife.

To make the jelly, reheat the poaching liquid until hot but not simmering, remove from the heat and add the gelatine. Stir, and pour into a bowl to chill for 4 hours.

Preheat the oven to 200°C/400°F/gas mark 6.

Melt the chocolate in a heatproof bowl suspended over a saucepan of barely simmering water.

Melt the butter and brush some of it over the inside of the dishes. Set aside the remainder.

Sift the flour into a bowl and then add the almonds, the remaining sugar and the salt. Whisk together the eggs, egg yolk and milk and add to the dry ingredients, whisking until smooth. Add the melted chocolate and remaining butter and stir until fully incorporated.

Divide the mixture between the two dishes, then place the pear halves with the thinner end facing inwards around the dish, with some of the pears face up and some face down.

Bake for 20 minutes. A skewer inserted in the clafoutis will not come out clean; it is important that it remains slightly gooey.

Serve hot or cold with crème fraîche and the red wine and pear jelly.

HINT: A melon baller is perfect for removing the core from a pear.

MAGIC

Launceston Place is a calm and friendly restaurant tucked away in Kensington, London. They gave us this recipe in the early 1990s, when they first discovered Green & Black's chocolate.

CHOCOLATE
BERRY TORTE

Preparation time: 25 minutes
Cooking time: 40 minutes
Use: 18–20cm, 6cm deep (7$\frac{1}{2}$–8in, 2$\frac{1}{2}$in deep) cake tin
Serves: 6

TORTE

25g (1oz) plain flour

5 teaspoons cocoa powder

75g (3oz) dark chocolate,
minimum 60% cocoa solids, broken into pieces

25g (1oz) unsalted butter

5 teaspoons double cream

4 egg whites

3 egg yolks

3 tablespoons caster sugar

250g (9oz) fresh blueberries or raspberries

125ml (4fl oz) whipping cream, to serve

ICING

100g (3$\frac{1}{2}$oz) dark chocolate,
minimum 60% cocoa solids, broken into pieces

50g (2oz) unsalted butter

3 tablespoons double cream

1 teaspoon icing sugar

Preheat the oven to 140°C/275°F/gas mark 1. Butter and line the cake tin with greaseproof paper.

Sift together the flour and cocoa and set aside.

Melt the chocolate in a heatproof bowl suspended over barely simmering water. Remove from the heat, add the butter and the cream, and stir well until the mixture is quite liquid.

Whisk the egg whites until stiff peaks form, add the sugar and continue to whisk until thick and glossy. Beat together the egg yolks and then gently fold in the flour and cocoa mixture. Add the melted chocolate and mix well. Spoon a few dollops of egg white into mixture, stir, then gently fold in the remainder of the egg whites.

Gently pour half the mixture into the prepared cake tin, dot half the berries evenly over it, then pour the rest of the mixture on top of the berries.

Bake for 35–40 minutes, until a skewer inserted into the centre of the cake comes out clean. Cool in the tin for 5 minutes and unmould on to a wire rack to cool.

To make the icing, melt the chocolate in a heatproof bowl suspended over a saucepan of barely simmering water. Remove from the heat, stir in the butter, cream and icing sugar. Immediately pour over the cake to coat it completely, smoothing the icing using a palette knife. Leave for 1 hour to harden.

Serve with whipped cream and the remaining berries.

HINT: Do not refrigerate this cake once you have iced it
as the icing will lose its shine and become dull and lifeless.

Gerard Coleman and Anne Weyns are the founders of L'Artisan du Chocolat, the most elegant chocolate shop in London. This recipe, which adds rock salt to the caramel, reflects their expertise in searching for and identifying unusual flavours that enhance good-quality chocolate.

CHOCOLATE AND SALTED CARAMEL
TART

Preparation time: 1 hour
Cooking time: 25 minutes
Use: 29cm (11in) loose-based tart tin
Serves 12–14

PASTRY

350g (12oz) plain flour

75g (3oz) icing sugar

125g (4½ oz) unsalted butter, cold

2 eggs

CARAMEL

45g (1½ oz) glucose syrup

275g (10oz) sugar

150ml (5fl oz) double cream

1 level teaspoon rock salt

25g (1oz) unsalted butter, diced

GANACHE

400ml (14fl oz) double cream

45ml (1½ fl oz) honey

350g (12oz) dark chocolate, minimum 60% cocoa solids, chopped

175g (6oz) unsalted butter, diced

To make the pastry, sift together the flour and icing sugar and cut the butter into chunks. Place in the food-processor and process, adding in the eggs at the end, until a dough forms. Roll out the pastry using quite a lot of flour as it can stick easily. Place it carefully into the tart tin. Chill in the fridge for about 30 minutes. Preheat the oven to 180°C/350°F/gas mark 4.

Blind-bake the pastry by covering it with greaseproof paper or baking parchment, filling with baking beans and cooking for about 15–20 minutes. Remove the beans and paper and continue to cook the pastry case for a further 10 minutes or until it has developed a light golden colour. Remove and leave to cool.

To make the caramel, pour the glucose syrup into a deep saucepan and bring to the boil. Add the sugar, gradually stir and continue to cook until the sugar has started to caramelise and turned a golden brown colour. At the same time, in a separate saucepan, bring the cream and salt to the boil. Remove the caramel from the heat and very carefully add the cream to the caramel, but be extremely careful as the mixture will rise rapidly in the saucepan and could cause serious burns. Using a hand-blender, mix until smooth over a low heat. Remove from the heat, add the diced butter and stir before pouring into the cooled pastry case.

To make the ganache, bring the cream and honey to the boil and pour over the chopped chocolate. Mix carefully with a spatula, working from the centre outwards. Once the mixture has cooled a little add the diced butter, and stir gently until the butter has melted. Pour the ganache on top of the caramel and leave to set in a cool place for about 4–6 hours.

HINT: This sweet pastry shrinks a lot, so when you place the pastry in the tin, make sure it reaches high up the sides of the tin.

Our English 'biscuit' and Italian *biscotti* are both words that derive from the Latin *biscoctus* meaning 'twice-cooked'. Large glass jars of biscotti often grace the counters of Italian coffee shops and usually the biscotti have almonds or hazelnuts in them. They should always be cut at an angle, shaped like a half-moon and are the perfect partner for a liqueur or a fruity dessert.

MAYA-DUNKED
BISCOTTI

Preparation time: 20 minutes
Cooking time: 45 minutes
Makes: 12

200g (7oz) plain flour

60g (2¹/₂ oz) cocoa powder

³/₄ teaspoon baking powder

pinch of salt

225g (8oz) caster sugar

³/₄ tablespoon ground espresso coffee

60g (2¹/₂ oz) dark chocolate, minimum 60% cocoa solids, chopped

2 medium eggs

1 medium egg yolk

³/₄ teaspoon vanilla extract

200g (7oz) Maya Gold chocolate, or other good-quality orange dark chocolate, broken into pieces

Preheat the oven to 180°C/350°F/gas mark 4. Cover a baking tray with greaseproof paper.

Sift together the flour, cocoa, baking powder, salt and caster sugar and place into the food-processor. Add the ground coffee and the dark chocolate. Using the pulse button, pulse until finely ground. Whisk together the eggs and yolk, add the vanilla extract and slowly add to the ground mixture, processing until the mixture forms a ball.

Lightly flour the work surface and roll the dough into a log. Flour the surface of the log ensuring it is coated on all sides. Place it on the baking tray. Bake the log for 25–30 minutes, then remove from the oven and reduce the temperature to 150°C/300°F/gas mark 2.

Remove the greaseproof paper with the log on it from the baking tray and leave to cool. Use a sharp knife to cut across the log at an angle to make slices about 1cm (¹/₂ in) thick. Place the slices on to the baking tray and bake for about 30 minutes until firm. Allow to cool.

Melt the chocolate in a heatproof bowl suspended over a saucepan of barely simmering water. Dip one end of each biscotti into the chocolate and place on a wire rack to set.

HINT: You can use any of your favourite types of chocolate to coat the biscotti.

A hybrid of two of our favourite recipes, this mousse looks beautiful and tastes heavenly, but it does take hours to make, however, and produces piles of washing up, so be prepared. Not for the faint-hearted!

WHITE & DARK CHOCOLATE MOUSSE
WITH RED BERRY COULIS

Preparation time: 20 minutes for each mousse
Chilling time: 2 hours for the dark mousse and then overnight for the white and dark mousse
Use: 18cm (7in) bottomless ring mould
Serves: 8–10

DARK CHOCOLATE MOUSSE

100g (3^1/$_2$ oz) dark chocolate,
minimum 60% cocoa solids, broken into pieces

40g (1^1/$_2$ oz) icing sugar

80g (3^1/$_4$ oz) unsalted butter, softened

3 large eggs, separated

40g (1^1/$_2$ oz) cocoa powder

pinch of salt

100ml (3^1/$_2$ fl oz) whipping cream

WHITE CHOCOLATE MOUSSE

200g (7oz) good-quality white chocolate,
broken into pieces

2 leaves gelatine

300ml (^{1}/$_2$ pint) whipping cream

3 large egg yolks

125g (4^1/$_2$ oz) icing sugar

2 tablespoons water

2 tablespoons Grand Marnier

RED BERRY COULIS

225g (8oz) strawberries or raspberries

40g (1^1/$_2$ oz) icing sugar

TO DECORATE

4 tablespoons of cocoa powder or

2 punnets of fresh raspberries

To make the dark chocolate mousse, melt the chocolate in a large heatproof bowl suspended over a saucepan of barely simmering water. Add the icing sugar and stir in the butter, then beat in the egg yolks and the cocoa and salt.

Whisk the egg whites until stiff peaks start to form. Separately whip the cream until thick, then gently fold the egg whites and the cream alternately into the chocolate mixture. Do not overmix, but ensure that the mixture is well blended.

Place the ring mould on a large, round serving plate. Pour the mousse into the mould and chill for about 2 hours before making the white chocolate mousse.

To make the white chocolate mousse, melt the chocolate in a large heatproof bowl suspended over a saucepan of barely simmering water. Ensure that the water does not touch the base of the bowl as white chocolate is especially sensitive to being overheated. Dissolve the gelatine in about four tablespoons of cream that has been warmed in a saucepan.

Whisk the egg yolks and icing sugar until thick and creamy and then add the Grand Marnier, the gelatine and cream mixture and the melted chocolate.

HINT: This mousse should be refrigerated before serving, especially on a hot day, but don't add the cocoa powder and coulis until you are ready to serve.

Whip the remainder of the cream until thick and fold it into the chocolate mixture.

Pour the white mousse on top of the dark mousse that has already set and chill overnight.

To make the coulis, purée the berries in a blender and then pass through a sieve into a bowl. Stir in the icing sugar to taste.

To unmould the mousse, dip a palette knife in boiling water, dry it, then slide it around the inside edge of the mould. Lift the ring mould off carefully and smooth the sides of the mousse with the palette knife.

To serve, sieve the cocoa over the top of the mousse to cover or scatter with whole raspberries. Pour some of the coulis on to the plate around the edge of the mousse and serve the remainder from a jug. Slice the mousse using a palette knife dipped in hot water.

MAGIC

Micah Carr-Hill has the coveted job of chocolate taster at Green & Black's and is the creative genius behind our products. He also loves to educate those around him in the art of eating and often arrives at work with anything from stuffed ox cheeks to Portuguese custard tarts. These ice cream balls are a variation on a recipe he created for one of our ice-cream promotions.

DEEP-FRIED CHOCOLATE NUT

ICE CREAM BALLS

Preparation time: 30 minutes
Freezing time: 30 minutes
Frying time: 90 seconds per 3 balls
Use: Ice-cream scoop, non-stick baking tray that fits in the freezer, a deep-fat fryer or deep saucepan
Makes: 10

500ml (18fl oz) tub good-quality dark chocolate ice cream

1 pack of filo pastry (30 sheets)

1 large egg yolk

100ml (3½ fl oz) milk

1–2 litres (1¾–2½ pints) sunflower or rapeseed oil for deep-frying

1 teaspoon icing sugar

100g (3½ oz) hazelnuts, chopped and toasted

50g (2oz) dark chocolate, minimum 60% cocoa solids

Take a tub of dark chocolate ice cream out of the freezer and leave it to soften for 10 minutes. Scoop into balls using an ice-cream scoop dipped in hot water, place them on a non-stick baking tray and return to the freezer for half an hour to harden.

Meanwhile prepare the pastry. Cut the filo pastry into 12cm (5in) squares (you will need 30). Make an egg wash by whisking together the egg yolk, milk and icing sugar. Take a square of filo pastry, brush it with egg wash and sprinkle the hazelnuts over it. Lay a second square over the first at an angle and repeat the brushing and sprinkling. Repeat the process with a final square. Continue until you have ten, triple layers of filo brushed with egg wash and sprinkled with nuts.

Preheat a heavy-based saucepan (or a deep-fat fryer), one-third filled with oil, to 180°C/350°F.

Take the ice cream balls out of the freezer and place one in the centre of each triple layer of pastry. Carefully wrap the filo around the balls without tearing the pastry. If you are not deep-frying the balls straight away put them back in the freezer until you need them so that the ice cream does not melt.

Using a metal slotted spoon, put the wrapped balls into the hot oil (no more than three at a time to ensure the oil does not cool down too much) and fry until golden brown; this will take about 90 seconds. Remove and drain on kitchen paper. Serve immediately with shavings of dark chocolate.

HINT: Buy a deep-frying thermometer (they are not expensive) to ensure the temperature of the oil is hot enough. If the oil cools down it will soak into the filo and melt the ice cream rather than creating a crisp pastry with insulating air pockets.

Only make this cake for celebrations. It was created the night before a photographic shoot when we realised the front cover of a recipe leaflet we had designed needed a photograph of a taller cake. The base is our 'Dark Chocolate Mousse Cake' and the top is the 'Taillevent Terrine' recipe picked up in the Eighties from the great Parisian restaurant that bears the name.

MARQUISE
AU CHOCOLAT

Preparation time: 50 minutes
Cooking time: 40 minutes
Cooling time: 2 hours
Chilling time: overnight
Use: 23cm (9 in) springform tin with high sides and removable base
Makes: 15 small, rich, slices

CAKE BASE

melted butter for greasing

1 tablespoon ground almonds
plus extra for dusting the tin

300g (10$\frac{1}{2}$oz) dark chocolate, minimum 60% cocoa solids (or 200g/7oz dark chocolate, minimum 60% cocoa solids, and 100g/3$\frac{1}{2}$oz Maya Gold or good-quality dark orange chocolate), broken into pieces

275g (10oz) caster sugar

165g (5$\frac{1}{2}$oz) unsalted butter

pinch sea salt

5 large eggs

MOUSSE

250g (9oz) dark chocolate,
minimum 60% cocoa solids, broken into pieces

100g (3$\frac{1}{2}$oz) icing sugar

175g (6oz) unsalted butter

5 large eggs, separated

150ml ($\frac{1}{4}$pint) whipping cream

cocoa powder for dusting

Preheat the oven to 180°C/350°F/gas mark 4.

Brush the tin with melted butter and dust with the ground almonds, shaking off any excess.

To make the cake, melt the chocolate, caster sugar,

butter and salt in a large, heatproof bowl suspended over a saucepan of barely simmering water.

Whisk the eggs with the ground almonds and fold into the chocolate mixture off the heat. Continue to fold until the mixture thickens. Pour into the cake tin and bake for 35–40 minutes. Leave to cool in the tin for about 2 hours before starting the mousse.

To make the mousse, melt the chocolate in a large, heatproof bowl suspended over a saucepan of barely simmering water. Remove from the heat and add half the icing sugar, stir, then whisk in the butter. Whisk in the egg yolks, one at a time. Set the mixture aside.

Whisk the egg whites until stiff peaks start to form. Add the remaining icing sugar and continue to whisk until glossy. Whip the cream until stiff peaks form.

Add one-third of the egg whites to the chocolate mixture and carefully mix to blend. Gently fold in the remaining whites, alternating with the whipped cream. Do not overmix, but ensure that the mixture is well blended. Pour the mousse over the cooled cake base in the cake tin and refrigerate overnight.

Remove the tin from the refrigerator about 15 minutes before serving. Dip a palette knife into boiling water, dry it and slide it round the sides of the cake to loosen it from the tin, then remove the ring. Re-heat the palette knife in boiling water, dry it and gently smooth the sides of the mousse.

Place the cake, still on the tin base, on to a large round serving plate. Dust generously with cocoa powder just before serving. Serve with crème fraîche or a custard sauce (see page 61).

You must have had people ask you whether you have tried Nigella Lawson's Clementine Cake? It is one of those recipes that fans of Nigella always mention and is so incredibly easy to make, it never fails. It is also the perfect partner for some melted Maya Gold Chocolate, especially at Christmas time when clementines are at their best.

NIGELLA'S

CLEMENTINE CAKE

Preparation time: 15 minutes
Cooking time: 2 hours to cook the clementines, 1 hour to bake the cake
Use: 20cm (8in) springform cake tin

4–5 clementines, skin on, to weigh 375g (13 oz)

melted butter for greasing

6 large eggs

225g (8oz) sugar

250g (9oz) ground almonds

1 heaped teaspoon baking powder

100g (3½ oz) Maya Gold Chocolate,
or other good-quality dark orange chocolate

Put the clementines into a saucepan, cover with cold water, bring to the boil and simmer for about 2 hours. Drain and set aside to cool. Then cut each clementine in half and remove the pips. Then pulp everything — skins, pith, and the fruit in a food-processor.

Preheat the oven to 190°C/375°F/gas mark 5. Butter and line the cake tin with greaseproof paper.

Beat the eggs. Add the sugar, almonds and baking powder. Mix well, add the pulped clementines, then stir together. Pour the mixture into the cake tin and bake for 1 hour or until a skewer inserted into the centre of the cake comes out clean. Cover the cake with foil or greaseproof paper after about 40 minutes to prevent the top from burning. Remove from the oven and immediately grate the chocolate over the top of the cake while still in the tin. Leave to cool completely. Remove from the tin and store in an airtight container.

HINT: Don't be tempted to serve this cake warm. It must only be eaten once it has cooled as the texture becomes moist and the flavours of the almonds and oranges have taken hold. It is best served the day after it is made.

Paul and Jeanne Rankin met while they were both travelling the world. Their passion for food grew while working in restaurant kitchens when funds ran out, and after training at Albert Roux's La Gavroche, they opened Roscoff in Belfast, which went on to win a Michelin star. Their latest restaurant, Cayenne, specialises in food with a hint of spice.

WHITE CHOCOLATE AND HAZELNUT CHEESECAKE
WITH ORANGE CARAMEL SAUCE

Preparation time: 1 hour
Cooking time: 1½ hours
Cooling time: at least 3 hours or overnight
Use: 23cm (9in) springform tin
Serves: 10–12

BASE

150g (5oz) Rich Tea biscuits

1 tablespoon sugar

3 tablespoons unsalted butter, melted

FILLING

75g (3oz) hazelnuts

75g (3oz) sugar

1kg (2¼lb) cream cheese

4 large eggs

1 large egg yolk

1 vanilla pod, split lengthways,
or 1 teaspoon vanilla extract

1 tablespoon Amaretto

pinch of freshly grated nutmeg

300g (11oz) good-quality white chocolate,
broken into pieces

icing sugar for dusting

ORANGE CARAMEL SAUCE

500ml (18fl oz) orange juice

40g (1½oz) sugar

1½ teaspoons arrowroot

2 tablespoons Grand Marnier

Preheat the oven to 200°C/400°F/gas mark 6.

To make the base, grind the biscuits to a fine texture in a blender or food-processor. In a bowl, combine the biscuits with the sugar and melted butter. Press the mixture on to the base of the springform tin.

To make the filling, roast the hazelnuts on a dry baking tray in the oven for 10–15 minutes until golden, then rub off their skins. Reduce the oven to 150°C/300°F/gas mark 2. Put the sugar with 2 tablespoons water in a pan and heat gently to dissolve, then boil until it is a rich caramel colour. Place the hazelnuts on an oiled tray and pour the caramel on top. Leave to harden, then break into pieces and pulse in a food-processor until coarsely ground. Set aside.

Pulse the cream cheese in a food-processor until smooth, then work in the eggs and egg yolk, the seeds scraped from the vanilla pod or the vanilla extract, Amaretto and nutmeg. Process until smooth. Melt the white chocolate in a heatproof bowl suspended over a saucepan of barely simmering water, ensuring that the water does not touch the base of the bowl. Add the melted chocolate to the mixture and, finally, the ground hazelnuts. Pour the mixture on to the base and bake for about 1½ hours until lightly set. Switch off the oven and leave to go cold and set. Remove from the oven and dust with icing sugar.

To make the Orange Caramel Sauce, put the orange juice in a saucepan and boil rapidly to reduce it by one third. Put the sugar with 1 tablespoon water in a pan and heat gently to dissolve, then bring to the boil and boil until it is a rich caramel colour. Reduce the heat, pour the juice on to the caramel and simmer until dissolved. Blend the arrowroot with a little water to make a smooth paste, then stir into the orange caramel until the mixture has thickened. Pass through a fine sieve and stir in the liqueur. Leave to cool.

To serve, pour some sauce on to individual plates and place a slice of cake in the centre.

My daughter Chloë is 6 years old and loves to dig into a wobbly soufflé. She also loves to eat her grandfather's speciality, perfectly ripe, sliced mangoes marinated in orange juice. This recipe with its chocolate edges is the one she asks for on special occasions.

MANGO, ORANGE AND LEMON
SOUFFLÉS

Preparation time: 1 hour 20 minutes
Cooking time: 10 minutes
Use: 8 ramekins
Serves: 8

255g (9oz) tinned mango slices

125g (4¹/₂ oz) dried mangoes

75ml (3fl oz) freshly squeezed orange juice

finely grated rind of 2 lemons

45g (1¹/₂ oz) melted butter for brushing ramekins

150g (5oz) dark chocolate,
minimum 60% cocoa solids, finely grated

250ml (9fl oz) full-cream milk

60g (2¹/₂ oz) unsalted butter

3 tablespoons flour

6 large eggs, separated

100g (3¹/₂ oz) caster sugar

Sieve the mangoes, draining the juice into a saucepan. Add the dried mangoes to the juice in the saucepan. Bring to simmering point and cook until the mangoes are tender and most of the liquid has been absorbed.

Put the contents of the saucepan, the reserved tinned mangoes and the orange juice into a blender or food-processor and whizz to a smooth purée. Stir in the lemon rind and leave to cool to room temperature.

Preheat the oven to 200°C/400°F/gas mark 6.

Brush the insides of the ramekins with the melted butter, then sprinkle on the grated chocolate, turning the dishes to ensure all the sides are evenly coated with a thick covering of chocolate. Tap out any excess and reserve for sprinkling over the finished soufflés. Place the ramekins on a baking tray to make it easier to remove them from the oven.

Heat the milk in a small saucepan. In a large saucepan melt the butter, then remove from the heat and stir in the flour. Return to a low heat and cook, stirring for a few minutes. When the roux starts to foam, gradually whisk in the milk. Cook over a moderate heat for a further few minutes until thickened. Remove from the heat and leave to cool before whisking in the egg yolks, one at a time. Leave to cool completely and then stir in the mango and orange purée.

Whisk the egg whites until soft peaks form. Gradually whisk in the caster sugar and continue to whisk until the meringue is firm. Stir a generous spoonful of meringue into the mango mixture to lighten it, then gently fold the mango mixture into the remaining meringue.

Fill the ramekins and bake for 8–10 minutes. Do not overfill the soufflés or they will tip over and collapse. Also remember never to open the oven door; if you don't have a light in your oven, peep at them but try not to let too much air into the oven. The soufflés will rise dramatically.

Carefully remove the soufflés from the oven and sprinkle the reserved grated chocolate over the top. Using a fish slice, lift the dishes on to small dessert plates and serve at once before they collapse.

TIME TO SHINE

The Toledo Cocoa Growers Association (TCGA) is a cooperative of 172 subsistence farmers.
Most are Maya people, who grow cacao for us in Belize. The fairtrade contract and the premium price
they can command for their organic cacao ensure that they have a stable economic future.

Don't be afraid: like so many of the pastry chef's techniques this cake is incredibly easy once you know how and always looks spectacularly impressive even if your piping goes a bit wobbly. The French call it a '*damier*' which means 'chequerboard'. This is a tall, three-layered cake and when cut each slice is a chequerboard of chocolate and vanilla.

CHEQUERBOARD

Preparation time: 20 minutes
Cooking time: 20 minutes
Use: 3 x 20 x 20cm (8 x 8in) cake tins, 2 x pastry bags with 2.25cm (³/₄ in) plain or fluted nozzles.
Serves: 8–10

VANILLA BATTER

225g (8oz) unsalted butter

225g (8oz) caster sugar

4 large eggs

1 teaspoon vanilla extract

250g (9oz) plain flour

10g (¹/₂ oz) baking powder

CHOCOLATE BATTER

225g (8oz) unsalted butter

225g (8oz) caster sugar

4 large eggs

220g (7¹/₂ oz) plain flour

50g (2oz) cocoa powder

10g (¹/₂ oz) baking powder

SUGAR SYRUP

250g (9oz) granulated sugar

300ml (¹/₂ pint) water

1 tablespoon rum

2 tablespoons apricot jam

GANACHE

150g (5oz) dark chocolate,
minimum 60% cocoa solids, broken into pieces

150ml (¹/₄ pint) whipping cream

Preheat the oven to 190°C/375°F/gas mark 5.

Butter the cake tins, line the bases with rounds of waxed paper, then butter the paper.

Begin by making the sugar syrup. Put the sugar and water in a saucepan and bring to the boil, without stirring, and boil until it begins to thicken. Remove from the heat and add the rum. Set aside.

To make the vanilla batter, cream together the butter and caster sugar thoroughly.

Add the eggs, one by one, mixing well between each addition, then add the vanilla extract.

Sift together the flour and baking powder and add to the mixture, stirring well. The mixture will be quite stiff. Set aside while you make the second batch.

To make the chocolate batter, cream together the butter and the caster sugar thoroughly. Add the eggs, one by one, mixing well between each addition.

Sift together the flour, cocoa and the baking powder and add to the mixture, stirring well. The mixture will be quite stiff.

Place the piping nozzles securely in the pastry bags. Put all the vanilla mixture into one of the bags and the chocolate mixture into the other. Place the three prepared baking tins in a row.

Starting with the vanilla batter, pipe a ring of vanilla batter inside the outer rim of one of the cake tins.

HINT: This cake becomes even more indulgent if you chop up a bar of our Almond Milk Chocolate into tiny pieces and sprinkle it over the top.

Then pipe a ring of chocolate batter inside the vanilla ring. Continue to pipe alternating rings of vanilla and chocolate batter. There should be 6 rings of alternating batter, the centre one being chocolate. Fill the second cake pan in the same way.

Fill the third cake tin, starting with a chocolate ring and ending with a vanilla ring.

Tap the base of each of the cake tins gently on a flat surface to release any air pockets before placing in the oven. Bake for about 20 minutes.

Remove the cakes from the oven, leave in their tins for 5 minutes to cool slightly. Turn them out on to a wire cooling rack and brush the sugar syrup over the bottom of each cake. Allow to cool.

Melt the chocolate in a heatproof bowl suspended over a saucepan of barely simmering water. Set aside.

Whip the cream until soft peaks form, then pour the hot chocolate over it in a steady stream, continuing to whip the cream, until the chocolate is just blended.

Once cool, place one of the cakes with a vanilla outer ring on a serving plate, spread apricot jam over the cake and then place the cake that has the chocolate outer ring on top of it. Spread apricot jam over it, then place the third cake on the top.

Using a palette knife, spread the ganache over the top and sides of the cake to cover it completely.

Amanda Allen has always enjoyed trying recipes from historical cookbooks and has found some intriguing combinations in medieval cookery. She adapted this recipe from Valentina Harris's book, *Regional Italian Cookery*. If you like a strong gamey flavour, you will love this dish, which was invented for the wedding of Caterina de Medici in the early sixteenth century and is typical of the flavours of the time.

TUSCAN SWEET AND SOUR

HARE

Preparation time: 30 minutes
Cooking time: 2 hours
Serves: 4–6

1 large hare

5 cloves garlic

2 sprigs rosemary

5 tablespoons extra virgin olive oil

2 onions, chopped

2 carrots, chopped

1 fennel bulb, chopped

handful parsley

handful basil

3 bay leaves

6 sage leaves

300ml (½ pint) Chianti

600ml (1 pint) game stock

110g (4oz) pine kernels

50g (2oz) sultanas

50g (2oz) candied peel

1 tablespoon granulated sugar

3 cavalluci or almond biscuits, ground

50g (2oz) dark chocolate, minimum 60% cocoa solids

3 tablespoons red wine vinegar

Cut the hare into joints. Peel and crush the garlic. Briefly fry the hare and half the garlic and rosemary with two tablespoons of oil in a flameproof casserole. Remove from the pan with a slotted spoon, discard the garlic and rosemary, and set the hare aside.

Heat the remaining oil in another dish and fry the onions, carrots, fennel, herbs and the rest of the garlic for 10 minutes.

Add the hare to the vegetables and herbs, brown on all sides, then add the wine and heat for a few minutes. Add the game stock, then cover and cook on a low heat for 1 hour and 30 minutes.

In another saucepan, mix together the pine kernels. sultanas, peel, sugar, cavalluci, chocolate and 8 tablespoons water. Heat for 10 minutes over a low heat, then remove from the heat and add the vinegar. Pour into the hare casserole, stir, then cook for a further 10 minutes.

HINT: This dish is best if left to cool overnight and then reheated the next day as this gives the rich flavours time to infuse and develop.

Chocolate Eruptions was one of the Groucho Club's signature dishes when they first gave it to us many years ago. The Groucho Club is a members-only restaurant and bar in London's West End and it is a favourite with the media, artists and writers.

CHOCOLATE
ERUPTIONS

Freezing time: 9 hours
Preparation time: 1 hour
Cooking time: 25–30 minutes
Use: 1 medium-sized bowl, 1 baking tray small enough to fit into your freezer
and 4 metal cake rings 65mm (2$\frac{1}{2}$in) in diameter.
Serves: 4

SAUCE

40g (1$\frac{1}{2}$oz) milk chocolate,
preferably 34% cocoa solids, broken into pieces

50ml (2fl oz) double cream

1 tablespoon water

10g ($\frac{1}{2}$oz) unsalted butter

PIE

melted butter for greasing

115g (4oz) dark chocolate,
minimum 60% cocoa solids, broken into pieces

50g (2oz) unsalted butter

100g (3$\frac{1}{2}$oz) caster sugar

2 large eggs, separated, and at room temperature

40g (1$\frac{1}{2}$oz) rice flour

40g (1$\frac{1}{2}$oz) ground almonds

Melt all the ingredients for the sauce in a saucepan over a low heat.

Pour into a freezerproof dish so that the mixture is about 15mm (1in) deep. Freeze for about 6 hours or until solid.

Brush a baking tray and the cake rings with the melted butter.

Melt the chocolate in a heatproof bowl suspended over a saucepan of barely simmering water.

Whisk together the butter and sugar until thick and creamy, then add the egg yolks, whisking them into the mixture.

Fold in the rice flour and the almonds, then mix in the melted chocolate. Whisk the egg whites until stiff peaks form and fold them gently into the mixture.

Place the rings on the baking sheet and use a spoon to fill them a quarter full with the pie mixture.

Remove the frozen sauce from the freezer. Using a mini metal cutter, cut rounds 25mm (1in) in diameter from the frozen sauce and place in the centre of each ring. Cover with the pie mixture to the rim of the ring and then level off with a palette knife. Freeze for at least 3 hours.

Preheat the oven to 180°C/350°F/gas mark 4. Remove the baking tray from the freezer and put straight in the oven. Bake for 25–30 minutes.

Leave the tray to cool for 5 minutes before scraping the excess off the rings. Turn the pies on their sides and gently push the rings off at the base.

Serve warm on individual plates.

HINT: Serve with icing sugar, fresh orange segments or crème fraîche.
Plan in advance and you could serve these with a dusting of pulverised, crystallised orange peel.
You'll find the recipe on page 181.

Delicious as a filling for pancakes, heated as a sauce with ice cream or on your toast at breakfast, this sophisticated variation on chocolate spread also makes a lovely gift.

PEAR & CHOCOLATE
SPREAD

Preparation time: 20 minutes
Chilling time: overnight
Cooking time: 40 minutes–1 hour
Use: heavy-based saucepan, 2–3 x 340g (12oz) preserving jars, wax paper circles
Makes: 840g (1³/₄ lb)

1.3kg (3lb) William pears, ripe but firm

750g (1³/₄ lb) granulated sugar

juice of 1 large orange

juice of 1 lemon

250g (9oz) dark chocolate,
minimum 60% cocoa solids, chopped

Peel the pears, cut them into quarters and remove the cores. In a large heavy-based saucepan mix the sugar with the orange and lemon juices, add the pears and mix together carefully.

Heat gently until the mixture begins to simmer and then remove from the heat and pour into a bowl. Add the chopped chocolate and mix until the chocolate has melted. Cover the bowl with greaseproof paper, allow to cool, and then place in the fridge or leave in a cool place overnight.

Pour the mixture back into a heavy-based saucepan, bring to the boil and leave to bubble for about 40 minutes to 1 hour or until the mixture reaches 105°C/220°F on a sugar thermometer. (If you do not have one, test by dropping a little on to a cold plate. If it becomes thick and gelatinous it is ready.)

While the spread is bubbling wash the preserving jars, their lids and seals in warm soapy water, rinsing thoroughly. Sterilise your jars by immersing them fully in boiling water for 10 minutes. You can also sterilise the jars by washing them in the dishwasher.

Spoon the pear and chocolate spread into the jars to within 1cm (¹/₂ in) of the rim. Cover with a circle of wax paper and then immediately put the top on.

HINT: This spread can be stored for up to three months, but once opened, keep in the fridge.

The Lighthouse Bakery in Battersea, south-west London, makes British, European and American breads and pastries. Elizabeth Weisberg and Rachel Duffield rely on traditional methods of hand-moulding and use long fermentation to develop the full flavour of their dough. They only make Chocolate Bread on Fridays, and on Valentine's Day the bakery makes chocolate heart-shaped rolls.

LIGHTHOUSE

CHOCOLATE BREAD

Preparation: 30 minutes
Proving time: 3 hours
Cooking time: 40 minutes
Use: 1 large baking sheet
Makes: 2 small oval loaves

20g (1oz) fresh yeast
or 2¹/₂ teaspoons active dried yeast

325ml (11fl oz) warm water

125g (4¹/₂ oz) caster sugar

1 large egg yolk

25g (1oz) unsalted butter, softened

600g (1¹/₄ lb) unbleached white bread flour

10g (¹/₂ oz) salt

30g (1oz) cocoa powder

250g (9oz) dark chocolate,
minimum 60% cocoa solids, roughly chopped

1 egg yolk for glazing

Combine the yeast, water and a generous pinch of sugar in a bowl and set aside for 5–10 minutes until bubbly. Add the egg yolk and butter to the yeast mixture.

If using a freestanding mixer, place all the remaining ingredients in the bowl and mix with the paddle for 1 minute on low speed to combine. Add the yeast mixture and mix with the paddle until well blended. Switch to the dough hook and mix first on low speed and then on medium speed until the dough is smooth and elastic – this takes about 4 minutes in total. Add a little extra water if it looks too dry.

If working by hand, combine the dry ingredients in a separate bowl and mix briefly with a spoon to blend. Then add the dry ingredients to the yeast mixture in three batches, stirring well with a spoon between additions. Add the chocolate pieces last. Knead the dough on a lightly floured surface for 8–10 minutes until the dough is smooth and elastic. Add a little extra water if it looks too dry.

Place the dough in a lightly oiled bowl, cover with clingfilm and leave to prove for about 2 hours in a warm, draught-free area.

Turn out the dough on to a lightly floured board and punch down. Divide into two equal pieces and shape each into an oval. Place both ovals on a greased or parchment-lined baking sheet, cover with a damp tea towel, and leave to prove for about 1 hour, or until doubled in size.

Preheat the oven to 220°C/425°F/gas mark 7.

Beat the egg with a fork and brush over the surface of the loaves. Place them on the baking sheet and bake for 15 minutes. Lower the temperature to 190°C/375°F/gas mark 5 for a further 25 minutes. Watch the loaves carefully during the last 5 minutes to avoid scorching the tops. Cool on a wire rack.

HINT: To make the heart shapes roll the dough into long snakes about 3cm (1in) in diameter by 37cm (15in) long. Shape into hearts and snip into the top cleavage and inside curves of the heart shape before baking. Make sure you keep an eye on the cooking time as chocolate bread can be ruined easily if baked for too long.

Cocoa is ranked the third most-valued commodity in world food after sugar and coffee. As a result of the pressures of international markets to produce bulk chocolate, there is a wide variety of cocoa beans and, depending on the variety, where they are grown and how they are processed, they result in many different cocoa flavours.

Cocoa beans are classed as either bulk beans or fine beans. Fine beans are derived from the two best-quality varieties, Criollo and Trinitario. Bulk beans are mainly harvested from the Forastero variety.

The fruit of the cacao tree is an oval-shaped pod about the size of a rugby ball. It can grow as long as 35cm and weigh up to 1kg. When ripe, the pods can be a variety of colours: red, green, orange or purple.

The word 'cacao' (pronounced *kakow*) is derived from the name for the cacao tree, *Theobroma cacao*, and is the word we use before the beans have been fermented and dried. Once dried and ready for shipping, we use the term cocoa.

This wonderful dessert was sent to us by Anne-Marie Graepel. Her mother would rustle this up during the post-war food shortages and it is a delicious chocolate pudding that is simple to make using only store-cupboard ingredients. The batter can be refrigerated for up to three days.

CHOCOLATE
LAYERED PANCAKE

Preparation time: 30 minutes
Resting time: 2 hours
Cooking time: 40 minutes
Use: 19cm (8in) heavy pancake pan, 19–20cm (8–9in) round ovenproof dish,
about 4–5cm (1–2in) deep
Serves: 6–8

PANCAKE BATTER

150g (5oz) plain white flour

pinch of salt

50g (2oz) caster sugar

3 large eggs

500ml (18fl oz) milk

zest of 1 orange

100g (3$\frac{1}{2}$ oz) unsalted butter, melted

butter or oil for greasing

FILLING

300g (11oz) sultanas or raisins

1 tablespoon Cointreau

1 tablespoon water

2 heaped tablespoons cocoa powder

5 heaped tablespoons caster sugar

285g (10$\frac{1}{2}$ oz) apricot jam

50g (2oz) unsalted butter

200ml (7fl oz) single cream

Soak the sultanas or raisins in the Cointreau and water. Sift the flour and salt into a bowl, mix in the sugar and make a well in the centre. Whisk together the eggs, milk and orange zest and stir in the melted butter. Pour into the well and, using a whisk, slowly incorporate the flour mixture into the liquid, whisking until smooth and velvety. Pour into a jug and leave to rest in the fridge for 1–2 hours.

Before cooking the pancakes, whisk the batter again gently. It should have the consistency of double cream; if it is too thick add some milk. Rub a pancake pan with a little butter or oil and place over a medium heat. As soon as the butter begins to bubble pour in a ladleful of batter. Swirl it evenly around the pan and pour any excess batter back into the jug. You will probably need to throw away your first pancake. Once the pancake is a nice golden-brown colour on the underside, flip it over using a palette knife. You will need to keep oiling the pan after 2 or 3 pancakes. Pile them, unfolded, on a plate. You should end up with about 20 pancakes.

Preheat the oven to 180°C/350°F/gas mark 4. Butter the ovenproof dish.

To make the layers, mix together the cocoa and sugar. Build up 4 layers of pancake in the dish, sprinkling $\frac{1}{2}$ tablespoon of the cocoa and sugar mixture and 1 dessertspoon of the soaked sultanas and raisins between each layer.

Spread every fifth layer with apricot jam instead of the cocoa and soaked fruit. There should be about 4 jam layers by the time the pancake pile is complete.

When you get to the last pancake sprinkle the cocoa and sugar mixture over it and dot with slices of butter. Prick the pancake pile with a fork and, just before putting it in the oven, pour the cream over the top.

Bake in the oven for 15 minutes until the top layer is nicely crisp. Serve immediately, using a sharp knife to cut into slices.

Nora Carey's passion for preserving was ignited when she worked on the Time Life *Good Cook* series of books while working in London. Nora's food career has ranged from working with Sir Terence Conran at Butler's Wharf, London to Disneyland Resort Paris. Her book, *Perfect Preserves*, is a must for any gardener who loves to cook and is full of recipes for preserving and using preserves.

CHESTNUT AND CHOCOLATE
SOUFFLÉS

Preparation time: 2 hours including cooling time
Cooking time: 12 minutes
Use: 8 ramekins
Serves: 8

400g (14oz) brown sugar

100ml (3½ fl oz) water

400g (14oz) prepared chestnuts peeled and cooked in water (jars rather than tinned)

1 vanilla pod, split lengthwise

75ml (3fl oz) brandy

124g (4½ oz) caster sugar

400g (14oz) whole preserved chestnuts in vanilla syrup

200g (8oz) dark chocolate, minimum 60% cocoa solids, broken into pieces

250ml (9fl oz) full-cream milk

60g (2½ oz) unsalted butter

3 tablespoons flour

6 large eggs, separated

icing sugar for dusting

Heat the brown sugar with the water over low heat until it begins to boil, add the peeled chestnuts and the vanilla pod. Bring the mixture back to the boil and boil for about 3 minutes. Leave to cool for about 1 hour, then stir in the brandy. Cover with clingfilm and set aside until needed.

Preheat the oven to 200°C/400°F/gas mark 6. Brush the ramekins with melted butter and dust with sugar.

Halve the preserved chestnuts and divide them between the ramekins.

To make the soufflé, place the chocolate and the milk in a small saucepan over a low heat and stir regularly until the chocolate has melted. In a large saucepan melt the butter, stir in the flour and cook over a low heat, stirring, for about 2 minutes. When the roux starts to foam, gradually whisk in the chocolate mixture. Cook over a moderate heat, stirring, for a few minutes until it has thickened. Remove from the heat and leave to cool. Whisk the egg yolks, one at a time, into the mixture.

Whisk the egg whites until soft peaks form. Gradually whisk in the remaining caster sugar and continue to whisk until the meringue is firm.

Stir a generous spoonful of the meringue into the chocolate mixture to lighten it, then gently fold the chocolate mixture into the remaining meringue.

Fill the ramekin dishes and bake for 8–10 minutes. Do not overfill the soufflés or they will tip over and collapse. Also remember never to open the oven door; if you don't have a light in your oven, peep at them but try not to let too much air into the oven. The soufflés will rise dramatically. Dust with icing sugar and serve immediately before they collapse.

HINT: 'Conkers' are not edible so, if you are planning to gather your own chestnuts, ensure you have the edible variety (*Castanea sativa*), which have softer spikes than the horse chestnut. If you are roasting your own chestnuts, remember to cut an 'X' on the flat side before roasting to prevent explosions.

Lorna Wing is the queen of creative catering and first earned a name for herself doing witty canapés like mini fish and chips in dolly-sized cornets made out of the *Financial Times*. This is her twist on Sachertorte that we featured in our very first recipe leaflet in 1993. It has stood the test of time and is the most decadent we have tasted. It also improves over time and is at its best after one week, stored in an airtight container.

LORNA WING'S

SACHERTORTE

Preparation time: 15 minutes
Cooking time: 1 hour
Use: 23cm (9in) springform cake tin
Serves: 10

TORTE

melted butter for greasing

200g (7oz) dark chocolate,
minimum 60% cocoa solids, broken into pieces

6 eggs

310g (11oz) granulated sugar

150g (5oz) ground almonds

1¹/₂ teaspoons freshly ground coffee

6 tablespoons apricot jam

ICING

100g (3¹/₂ oz) dark chocolate,
minimum 60% cocoa solids, broken into pieces

40g (1¹/₂ oz) unsalted butter

Preheat the oven to 180°C/350°F/gas mark 4. Brush the tin with melted butter, then line it with greaseproof paper.

To make the torte, melt the chocolate in a heatproof bowl suspended over a saucepan of barely simmering water. Separate 5 of the eggs, then whisk the egg yolks, the whole egg and the sugar until the mixture is thick and creamy.

In a separate bowl whisk the egg whites until stiff peaks form.

Add the ground almonds, coffee grounds and melted chocolate to the egg yolk mixture and stir well. Gently fold in the egg whites and pour into the prepared tin.

Bake for 1 hour, covering the cake with foil after 40 minutes to prevent the top from burning. Check that a skewer inserted into the centre comes out clean and remove the cake from the oven. Release the spring-form ring and leave the cake on the base to cool on a wire rack.

Melt the apricot jam over a low heat, strain and then brush it over the cooled cake.

To make the icing, melt the chocolate in a heatproof bowl suspended over a saucepan of barely simmering water. Add the butter and stir until it has the consistency of thick pouring cream. Pour the icing evenly over the cake, smoothing it over the top and sides using the back of a teaspoon. Leave to set.

HINT: Make a pattern of rings on the top and around the sides of the cake using the back of a teaspoon and then pipe 'Sachertorte' in the traditional style.

This recipe comes from Elisabeth Luard, whose mouth-watering article about chocolate made it irresistible and reminds us that wild meat benefits from a sweet-sour marinade and long, gentle cooking. Agrodolce, or sweet-sour sauces, originated in Roman times, when honey, sweet wine, dried fruit, vinegar and spices were used to mask any unpleasant flavours from the meat, which was not always very fresh, and also to counteract the effects of preserving salt.

ITALIAN VENISON

AGRODOLCE

Preparation time: 40 minutes
Marinating time: 12 hours minimum
Cooking time: 2 hours
Serves: 6

1.5kg (3lb 5oz) venison (shoulder or haunch), cubed or cut into long strips

MARINADE

400ml (14fl oz) red wine

3 tablespoons red wine vinegar

3 tablespoons olive oil

1 carrot, chopped

1 large onion, sliced

1 celery stalk including the head, chopped

3 cloves garlic, crushed

sprig rosemary

sprig thyme

4 sage leaves

3 bay leaves

1 teaspoon juniper berries, crushed

$^1/_2$ teaspoon black peppercorns, crushed

CASSEROLE

3 tablespoons olive oil

100g (3$^1/_2$ oz) pancetta or dry-cure streaky bacon, diced

1 medium onion, very thinly sliced

1 tablespoon plain flour

1 tablespoon raisins

1 teaspoon ground cinnamon

$^1/_2$ teaspoon grated nutmeg

salt and pepper

1-2 tablespoons pine nuts

2-3 squares dark chocolate, minimum 60% cocoa solids

Put all the marinade ingredients into a large bowl and stir well. Add the prepared venison and stir, then leave in a cool place overnight, or preferably two nights.

Remove the meat from the marinade and pat dry with kitchen paper. Strain the marinade and set aside.

Preheat the oven to 150°C/300°F/gas mark 3.

Heat the oil in a flameproof casserole dish and gently fry the pancetta until the fat runs and it browns a little. Remove and set aside. In the same oil, brown the venison, in batches, to avoid overcrowding the pan. Remove and set aside. Add the onion, season lightly and cook until soft. Sprinkle in the flour until it absorbs some of the fat, scraping up the caramelised bits. Add the reserved marinade and the raisins, bring to the boil, then reduce the heat and stir until the sauce thickens and no longer smells of alcohol.

Return the pancetta and venison to the casserole, leave it to bubble up, then add the spices, the salt and the pepper.

Cover and cook in the oven for 1 hour 30 minutes, until the meat is soft enough to cut with a spoon. Add a little hot water every now and then if it looks as though it is drying out.

Toss the pine nuts in a dry pan over a low heat to toast.

When the meat is tender, stir in the dark chocolate and leave it to bubble up again until the sauce is thick and shiny.

TIME TO SHINE

If you like stollen you will adore this chocolate version created by Liz Usher, who had tried in vain to find a recipe for chocolate bread and decided to create one herself for our National Trust competition. This recipe came a close runner-up to the Chilean chocolate sausages on page 91.

MAYA GOLD
STOLLEN

Soaking time: 12 hours
Preparation time: 30 minutes
Proving time: 30 minutes
Cooking time: 35 minutes
Use: 30cm x 19cm (12in x 7½in) roasting tin
Serves: 10

75g (3oz) mixed dried fruit, chopped

25g (1oz) mixed peel, chopped

65ml (2½fl oz) dark rum

zest and juice of 1 orange

100g (3½oz) Maya Gold Chocolate,
or good-quality dark orange chocolate

50g (2oz) glacé cherries

DOUGH

375g (13oz) strong white flour

25g (1oz) cocoa powder

¼ teaspoon salt

½ teaspoon grated nutmeg

1 teaspoon mixed spice

2 teaspoons easy blend yeast

150ml (¼pint) milk

125g (4½oz) unsalted butter

50g (2oz) golden caster sugar

2 medium eggs

COCOA MARZIPAN

100g (3½oz) ground almonds

75g (3oz) icing sugar

25g (1oz) cocoa powder

DECORATION

40g (1½oz) icing sugar

25g (1oz) cocoa powder

Mix the mixed dried fruit and mixed peel in half of the rum and stir in the orange zest and juice. Leave to soak overnight.

Roughly chop the chocolate into small chunks and quarter the cherries. Mix with the soaked fruits.

To make the dough, begin by combining the flour, cocoa, salt, nutmeg, mixed spice and the yeast. Next, gently melt together the milk and 75g (3oz) of the butter, stir in the caster sugar until dissolved. Leave to cool. Separate one of the eggs, reserving the white. Beat the yolk with the other egg and whisk into the cooled milk mixture. Make a well in the centre of the dry ingredients, add the liquid and mix well.

Turn out and knead gently on a lightly floured board. Place in the bowl, cover with clingfilm and leave to rise in a warm place for 30 minutes while you make the marzipan.

Line the roasting tin with greaseproof paper.

Preheat the oven to 190°C/375°F/gas mark 5.

HINT: If you like a soft crust on your stollen, place a roasting tin filled with water in the bottom of your oven when you bake it. The steam produced will stop the crust from hardening.

To make the marzipan, mix together the ground almonds, icing sugar and cocoa with the reserved egg white. Knead lightly together in the bowl until a pliable ball forms. Roll out to an oblong about the length of the tin.

Melt together the remaining butter and rum.

Turn the dough out on to a lightly floured board. Knead a little, then roll it out into an oblong about 5mm (^{1}/$_4$ in) thick.

Brush the dough with some melted butter and rum. Place half the fruit mixture on the top two-thirds of the dough, then fold the bottom third, two-thirds of the way up the oblong, then fold down the top third over it. Seal the edges with the rolling pin. Turn the

dough clockwise so that the right-hand edge is now at the bottom, then roll it out into an oblong again. Brush again with the butter and rum and cover the top two-thirds with the remaining fruit mixture, fold, seal and roll again as before. Do not turn it this time.

Place the marzipan in the centre of the dough, fold in the two sides to meet in the centre and place, join-side down, in the lined tin. Brush the top with butter and rum and bake for 35 minutes.

As soon as you remove the stollen from the oven, brush with the remaining butter and rum mixture (which you may need to reheat slightly) and then dredge heavily with icing sugar. Allow to cool, then sprinkle with cocoa powder to serve.

MELTING

After they have been picked, the pods are carefully cut open with a machete to reveal up to
45 beans surrounded by a gooey, white pulp. The beans and pulp are then removed by hand.

This exquisite tart is from Sue Lawrence's *Book of Baking* which is full of amazingly original recipes including Haggis Bread and an irresistible Rhubarb and White Chocolate Tart.

CHOCOLATE-CRUSTED
LEMON TART

Preparation time: 40 minutes
Chilling time: 3 hours minimum
Cooking time: 35 minutes
Use: 23cm (9in) tart tin with removable base
Serves: 6

PASTRY

175g (6oz) plain flour

25g (1oz) cocoa

pinch of salt

25g (1oz) icing sugar

125g (4½oz) unsalted butter, chilled and diced

1 large egg yolk

2 tablespoons cold water

FILLING

75g (3oz) dark chocolate,
minimum 60% cocoa solids, grated

3 juicy unwaxed lemons

150g (5oz) caster sugar

4 large eggs

150ml (5oz) double cream

icing sugar to sprinkle

To make the pastry, sift together the flour, cocoa, salt and icing sugar. Rub in the cold butter using a food-processor or your fingertips until the mixture resembles fine breadcrumbs.

Mix the egg yolk with the water, and add to the mixture to make a dough. You may need a little more water. Gather the pastry into a ball, wrap it in grease-proof paper and chill in the fridge for about 1 hour.

Roll out the pastry from the centre and away from you, then back to the centre and down towards you, using your weight to push down on it to avoid stretching it. Line the tart tin.

Prick the pastry base with a fork in several places and chill for at least 2 hours or overnight.

Preheat the oven to 200°C/400°F/gas mark 6.

Line the pastry case with foil and baking beans and bake blind for 15 minutes, then remove the foil and beans and bake for a further 5 minutes. (Be careful not to overbake as the chocolate pastry can quickly develop a bitter taste.) Remove the tin from the oven and reduce the temperature to 160°C/325°F/gas mark 3.

While the pastry is still hot, scatter the grated chocolate evenly over the base and then leave to cool.

To make the filling, finely grate the zest from the lemons into a mixing bowl. Squeeze and strain the lemon juice and add it to the zest with the sugar. Whisk until the sugar has dissolved, then whisk in the eggs and the cream until the mixture is smooth.

Pour the filling into the cooled pastry case and carefully return it to the oven. Bake for 30–35 minutes until just set. Remove from the oven and leave on a wire rack to cool completely before removing from the tin.

Dust with icing sugar before serving.

HINT: If you love making pastry try to find yourself a rolling pin with ball bearings in it!
You can often pick up large, old ones at flea markets. They are the best
because they are heavy, so you don't have to put as much effort into rolling.

MELTING

The pulp that cocoons the deep beetroot, pink or white beans inside the pod is placed in wooden boxes and lined with banana leaves. They are then covered with more banana leaves and left for about five days to ferment.

The action of fermentation kills the beans and breaks down the sugars whilst other compounds and enzymes react together to produce the precursors of the first chocolate flavours.

Unfermented bulk beans are often used in cheaper chocolate blends where their poor taste can be disguised using further processing techniques and strong flavours.

Margaret Iveson is a bit of a chocolate addict, together with most of her family and many of her friends. As far as chocolate cakes go, she declares this one is one of the most satisfying and, she also claims, indestructible. Perfect for lazy days like Sundays.

SUNDAY
CHOCOLATE CAKE

Preparation time: 30 minutes
Baking time: 25 minutes
Use: 2 x 20cm (8in) cake tins

200g (7oz) plain flour

4 tablespoons cocoa powder

2 teaspoons baking powder

1 teaspoon bicarbonate of soda

1 teaspoon lemon juice

200ml (7fl oz) milk

100g (3½ oz) unsalted butter, softened

175g (6oz) caster sugar

2 large eggs, beaten

½ teaspoon vanilla extract

SYRUP

4 tablespoons apricot jam

2 tablespoons lemon juice

1 tablespoon kirsch

BUTTER CREAM FILLING

100g (3½ oz) dark chocolate, minimum 60% cocoa solids

50g (2oz) unsalted butter

100g (3½ oz) icing sugar

1 large egg yolk

ICING

50g (2oz) dark chocolate, minimum 60% cocoa solids

25g (1oz) unsalted butter

1 tablespoon rum

Preheat the oven to 190°C/375°F/gas mark 5. Butter and flour the cake tins.

Sift together the flour, cocoa, baking powder and bicarbonate of soda three times.

Stir the lemon juice into the milk to curdle it.

In a large bowl cream together the softened butter and sugar until fluffy. Beat in some of the egg, then some of the flour mixture, then some of the milk and lemon juice. Continue in this way, beating vigorously between each addition, until the batter is fairly stiff (don't add all the milk if it seems to be getting too liquid). Finally add the vanilla extract.

Divide the batter between the tins and bake for 20–25 minutes, until springy to the touch. Leave the cakes in their tins for a few minutes and then turn them out to cool on to a wire rack, so that the top crust is on the bottom. Prick the bases gently all over.

To make the syrup, simmer the jam, lemon juice and kirsch and pour it evenly over the cooled cakes.

For the Butter Cream Filling, melt the chocolate in a heatproof bowl suspended over a saucepan of barely simmering water and leave to cool until warm to touch while you cream together the butter and icing sugar. Beat in the egg yolk, then the chocolate, spread it on to the surfaces and sandwich the cakes together.

To make the icing, melt the chocolate as above, beat in the butter, then the rum and continue to beat until glossy. Leave to cool slightly before pouring over the top of the cake. Leave to set.

The only drink for a very hot summer's day or on a balmy night – sip and feel yourself cool down. Iced Mocha Coffee is also perfect as a dessert after a barbecue or *al fresco* lunch.

ICED

MOCHA

Preparation time: 15–20 minutes
Marinating time: 8 hours minimum, or up to 1 week
Chilling time: 2 hours
Makes: 6 tall glasses

200g (7oz) fresh cherries

300ml (½ pint) brandy or port

1 litre (1¾ pints) strong freshly ground filter coffee

8 tablespoons good-quality hot chocolate powder

6 tablespoons demerara sugar

500ml (18fl oz) dark chocolate ice cream

500ml (18fl oz) vanilla ice cream

250ml (9fl oz) double cream

cocoa powder or dark chocolate for sprinkling

Marinate the cherries in the brandy or port overnight or preferably for up to 1 week in the fridge.

Make the coffee and while it is still hot stir in the hot chocolate and the sugar to taste. Remember not to make the mocha too sweet as the ice cream will be an additional sweetener.

Chill the mocha in the fridge until very cold. Remove the ice cream from the freezer and leave it to soften for 10 minutes. Pour the mocha into six glasses, only three-quarters full, to allow enough room for 2 balls of ice cream.

Drop 3 or 4 marinated cherries into each glass and then, using an ice-cream scoop, carefully drop 1 ball of vanilla ice cream into the mocha, then 1 ball of chocolate ice cream on top. Try not to disturb the ice cream too much as it will cloud the lovely dark mocha coffee. Pour 1–2 tablespoons of double cream over the top of the ice cream and then sprinkle some cocoa or dark chocolate flakes over it. Serve immediately.

HINT: You can use left-over filter coffee, but if it has cooled, don't reheat it. Just pour a little hot water over the hot chocolate powder before you add it to the coffee. If it is an unbearably hot day put some ice cubes into the mocha before you add the ice cream.

Sylvia Sacco made this tiramisu for the end-of-filming party for Gilly Booth's film *One Dau Trois 123*, in which Sylvia played the leading lady. The recipe belongs to her mother, Sonia Nicastro, and lives up to its name, which means 'pick-me-up'. The exhausted film crew couldn't get enough of it and the recipe was immediately nabbed for this book.

SYLVIA'S

TIRAMISU

Preparation time: 25 minutes
Chilling time: minimum 2 hours or overnight
Use: 23cm (9in) serving dish, about 7cm (3in) deep
Serves: 6

200g (7oz) Savoiardi biscuits or ladyfingers

350ml (12fl oz) espresso or strong filter coffee

4 tablespoons Grand Marnier or Marsala

4 eggs, separated

125g (4$\frac{1}{2}$oz) granulated sugar

400g (14oz) mascarpone cheese

pinch of salt

2 tablespoons cocoa powder

Break the biscuits into two or three pieces and line the bottom of the serving dish with half of them. Spoon half the coffee over the biscuits and then drizzle with half of the liqueur.

Whisk together the egg yolks and sugar until thick and creamy, add the mascarpone cheese and stir well until smooth and thick. Whisk the egg whites until stiff peaks form and add a pinch of salt. Gently fold the egg whites into the mascarpone cheese and egg mixture.

Spoon half the mixture over the biscuits in the bottom of the dish. Place the remainder of the biscuits on top of the mixture, spoon the reserved coffee over them and then drizzle with the remaining liqueur. Cover with the remaining mascarpone cheese and egg mixture. Sift the cocoa powder evenly over the top.

Cover with clingfilm and chill for at least 2 hours, or preferably overnight.

HINT: Tiramisu is traditionally served in a glass bowl, but why not be adventurous and use a terracotta dish? It also looks beautiful in an old china vegetable serving dish.

Deryl Rennie made this loaf cake so that she could enjoy her two favourite flavours at once. The pieces of chocolate sink into the batter so that they embed themselves at the bottom of the loaf while the lemon gives the cake a refreshing edge.

LEMON DRIZZLE

WITH SUNKEN DARK CHOCOLATE CHUNKS

Preparation time: 15 minutes
Cooking time: 40 minutes
Use: 12 x 19cm (5 x 7in) loaf tin
Serves: 10

BATTER

125g (4$\frac{1}{2}$ oz) unsalted butter

125g (4$\frac{1}{2}$ oz) caster sugar

2 large eggs

150g (5oz) self-raising flour

1 teaspoon baking powder

grated rind of 1 large lemon

1 tablespoon milk

75g (3oz) dark chocolate, minimum 60% cocoa solids, chopped

LEMON DRIZZLE

50g (2oz) golden granulated sugar

juice of 1 lemon

Preheat the oven to 180°C/350°F/gas mark 4. Line the loaf tin with greaseproof paper.

Whisk the butter, caster sugar, eggs, flour, baking powder and lemon rind together for about 2 minutes. Whisk in the milk to make a soft dropping consistency. Stir in the chocolate.

Spoon the mixture into the prepared tin, smooth the surface, and bake for 40 minutes or until the centre of the cake springs back when gently pressed. Remove from the oven.

Stir the granulated sugar into the lemon juice and pour over the hot cake in its tin. Make a few holes with a fine skewer if the icing remains on the surface.

Remove the cake from its tin and place on a wire rack, leaving it in its paper to cool completely.

HINT: If you use grated chocolate, it will give the cake a speckly appearance.

A fun way to serve this sorbet is with a glass of coffee liqueur which can then be poured over the sorbet or drunk separately. It is equally delicious served with a delicate *crème anglaise* and perfectly ripe peaches, raspberries, oranges, nectarines or apricots and simple butter biscuits or tuiles.

CHOCOLATE

SORBET

Preparation time: 15 minutes
Freezing time: 3–4 hours
Use: ice-cream machine
Serves: 4

100g (3½ oz) dark chocolate,
minimum 60% cocoa solids, broken into pieces

100ml (3½ oz) water

60g (2½ oz) cocoa powder

SUGAR SYRUP

250ml (9fl oz) water

150g (5oz) caster sugar

To prepare the sugar syrup, put the sugar and the water into a saucepan and bring to the boil without stirring, leave to bubble for about 5 minutes or until the sugar has dissolved, then remove from the heat.

While the sugar syrup is bubbling, melt the chocolate in a heatproof bowl suspended over a saucepan of barely simmering water. Once it has melted, add the 100ml (3½ fl oz) water to the sugar syrup and reheat until warm, whisk in the cocoa, then add the melted chocolate, whisking together until smooth.

Churn in an ice-cream maker, following the manufacturer's instructions, until smooth.

HINT: It is a good idea to chill the sorbet down before churning it as it will set more quickly.
To do this, place it over a bowl of water filled with ice cubes and stir occasionally,
but be careful not to allow any of the water into the sorbet at this stage.

MELTING

There are few commercially made ice creams that are a patch on the home-made version and the key to this is in the stirring and cooling, as well as the ingredients. It is vital to have an ice-cream machine to achieve a thick, creamy texture and to use the best-quality eggs and dairy products.

ICE CREAM

Preparation time: 15 minutes
Chilling time: 10-20 minutes
Use: ice-cream maker
Serves: 6

250ml (9fl oz) full-cream milk

250ml (9fl oz) double cream

1 vanilla pod

3 large egg yolks

100g (3½ oz) caster sugar

Pour the milk and cream into a heavy-based saucepan. Split the vanilla pod lengthwise, scrape out the seeds and add both the pod and seeds to the milk and cream mixture. Bring to the boil, then remove from the heat, cover and leave to infuse for about 15 minutes. Strain the liquid.

Whisk together the egg yolks and caster sugar until thick and creamy. Continue to whisk as you pour over a little of the strained milk and cream, then add the rest of the milk and cream and whisk until well blended. Place the saucepan over a medium heat and, stirring frequently with a wooden spoon, cook until the custard has thickened and coats the back of the spoon. Then follow your chosen recipe below.

CHOCOLATE, HAZELNUT & CURRANT

100g (3½ oz) dark chocolate, minimum 60% cocoa solids, broken into pieces

100g (3½ oz) Hazelnut and Currant Chocolate, or other good-quality fruit and nut chocolate finely chopped

Melt the dark chocolate in a heatproof bowl suspended over a saucepan of barely simmering water and carefully stir into the custard.

Transfer to a metal bowl and place the bowl on a bed of ice in a little water to chill. Stir occasionally to prevent a skin from forming.

Once the mixture has cooled, transfer to an ice-cream machine and churn according to the manufacturer's instructions. Add the chunks of Hazelnut and Currant Chocolate just before the ice cream sets.

BUTTERSCOTCH BAR

100g (3½ oz) Butterscotch Chocolate, or any other flavoured bar, chopped into medium-sized chunks

Remove from the heat, transfer to a metal bowl and place it on a bed of ice and a little water to chill. Stir occasionally to prevent a skin from forming. Once the custard has cooled add the chunks of butterscotch chocolate, transfer to the ice-cream machine and churn according to the manufacturer's instructions.

SAUCES

BUTTERSCOTCH BAR

100g (3¹/₂ oz) Butterscotch Chocolate, broken into pieces

4 tablespoons milk

Melt the chocolate with the milk in a small saucepan over a very low heat until the chocolate and butterscotch pieces are melted and combined with the milk. Leave to cool for a few minutes and then pour over cake or use as a sauce for ice cream.

SIMPLE CHOCOLATE

100g (3¹/₂ oz) dark chocolate, minimum 60% cocoa solids, chopped

125ml (4fl oz) double or whipping cream

10g (¹/₂ oz) unsalted butter

Melt the chocolate with the cream in a heatproof bowl suspended over a saucepan of barely simmering water, stirring frequently. Once the chocolate has melted, add the butter and stir until it has melted. Serve warm.

ALISTAIR LITTLE'S CHOCOLATE FUDGE

125ml (4fl oz) double cream

140g (5oz) granulated sugar

25g (1oz) unsalted butter

75ml (3fl oz) golden syrup

75ml (3fl oz) milk

¹/₂ teaspoon vanilla essence

100g (3¹/₂ oz) dark chocolate, minimum 60% cocoa solids, broken into pieces

Put all the ingredients except the chocolate in a heavy-based saucepan over a moderate heat, stirring constantly until the mixture is a pale caramel colour. This will take about 10–15 minutes after coming to a slow boil. Remove from the heat and beat in the chocolate pieces. Stir in 35ml (1¹/₂ fl oz) of cold water. If the mixture is still too thick, continue adding water, a spoonful at a time, until you achieve a good pouring consistency. Serve immediately or keep warm in a bain marie until needed.

CUSTARD

1 vanilla pod

300ml (¹/₂ pint) full-cream milk

2 large egg yolks (3 if you want a very thick sauce)

1 heaped tablespoon caster sugar

Split the vanilla pod lengthwise, scrape out the seeds and put both pod and seeds in a saucepan together with the milk. Bring to the boil and then remove from the heat and leave to infuse for 15 minutes. Whisk together the egg yolks and the sugar until thick and creamy. Remove the vanilla pod and reheat the milk until it begins to boil, then whisk the boiling milk into the egg mixture. Return to the saucepan and heat gently, stirring all the time with a wooden spoon, until the sauce begins to thicken and dragging your finger or a knife across the back of the spoon leaves a clear trail. Remove the custard from the heat and pour into a bowl. Serve hot or chilled.

CUSTARD WITH MINT

Make the recipe as above but substitute the vanilla pod with a handful of chopped mint. Add Crème de menthe to taste once the custard has cooled a little.

LICKING THE BOWL

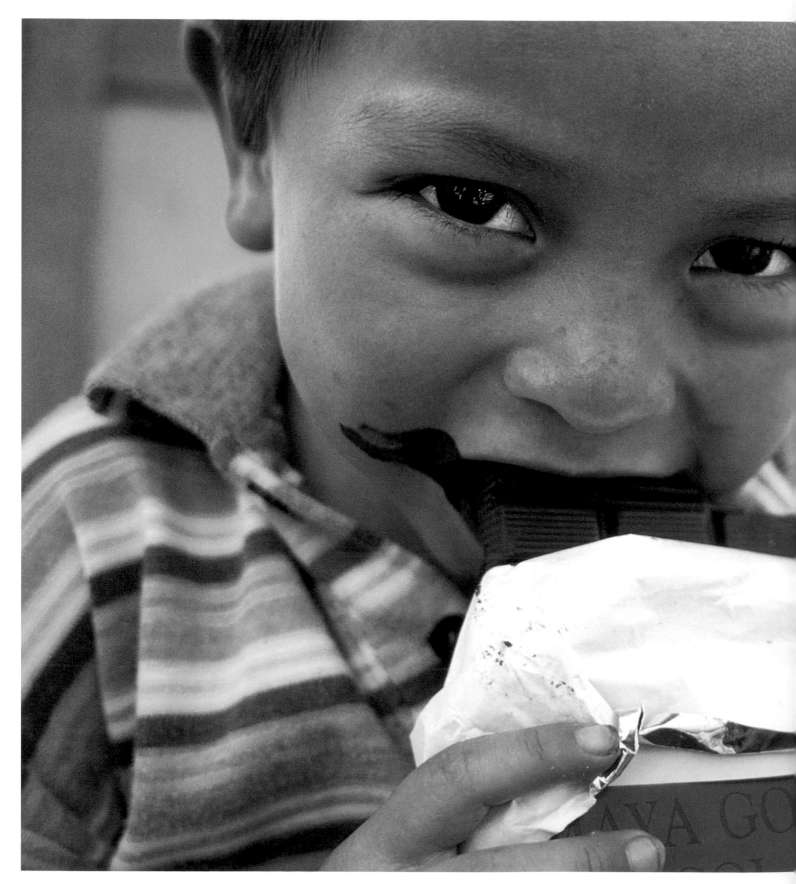

With the only secondary school far away in Punta Gorda, many cacao farmers' children have to board with families near the school. Without the extra income generated from Fairtrade organically grown cacao, their parents would not be able to afford the cost of their accommodation and the weekly bus fare.

Here is a good way to feed hordes of children a dessert that they all love without having piles of bowls to wash up. Make it extra naughty by filling the bottom with a surprise: jelly beans, Maltesers, Smarties, Rolos, silver balls, or any other chocolate sweet. Don't tempt them by telling them the surprise is there, otherwise they'll bite the bottom and you will wonder why you didn't give them the bowls!

FRUIT SPLIT

SURPRISE

Preparation time: 15 minutes
Use: a block of polystyrene to hold the dipped cones

milk chocolate bars, for dipping the cones

chopped nuts or silver balls or hundreds and thousands for coating the chocolate-dipped cones

quality wafer ice-cream cones

chocolate and vanilla ice cream

YOUR CHOICE OF:

melon, cut into tall slices

bananas, cut in half

pineapple, cut into long tall chunks

dragon fruit, sliced into quarters, skin on

kiwi fruit, sliced lengthwise

your choice of chocolate treat that will fit into the bottom of the cone

drinking chocolate powder to decorate

Remove the ice cream from the freezer and leave to soften for 10 minutes. Melt the chocolate in a heatproof bowl suspended over a saucepan of barely simmering water.

Dip the tops of the cones in the melted chocolate and then into the chopped nuts, silver balls or hundreds and thousands. Wedge the tip of the cone into a large piece of polystyrene to set.

Fill the cones with a few treats. Fill with softened ice cream down one side of the cone and then place your slices of fruit down the other side of the cone so that they stick out at the top. Wedge more ice cream into the cone to help hold the fruit up, then sprinkle with the chocolate powder.

HINT: You can make this treat even naughtier by wedging a chocolate finger,
flake or part of a honeycomb bar in the cone as well.

Bea Hovell is seven years old and she loves baking. She usually makes her Thumbprint Cookies with jam as a filling, but has found that our chocolate spread seems to be another perfect partner for them. Remember chocolate spread has hazelnuts in it so do be careful who you give them to!

BEA'S

THUMBPRINT COOKIES

Preparation time: 20 minutes
Resting time: 1 hour
Cooking time: 10–12 minutes
Makes: 18–24

175g (6oz) unsalted butter, softened

175g (60z) caster sugar

1 large egg

125g (4¹/₂oz) self-raising flour

175g (6oz) plain flour

200g (7oz) chocolate hazelnut spread

Line a baking sheet with greaseproof paper.

Cream the butter and sugar until light and fluffy using an electric mixer. Add the egg and beat well. Stir in the self-raising and the plain flour and mix to a dough. Leave to rest for 1 hour.

Preheat the oven to 180°C/350°F/gas mark 4.

Use the palms of your hands to roll about 1 heaped tablespoon of the dough into a ball about 2.5cm (1in) in diameter, then use the palm of your hand to flatten it on to the baking sheet. Press your thumb into the middle of the dough to make a hole. Continue with the rest of the dough, ensuring the cookies are spaced well apart as they will expand as they cook. Use a teaspoon to fill the hole with chocolate spread.

Bake for 10–12 minutes or until the cookies are golden. Cool on a wire rack.

HINT: Place a tea-towel under the bowl to prevent it from slipping while you are mixing and put four little dots of butter on to the baking tray before you line it with the greaseproof paper to stop the paper from shifting.

After fermentation, the beans are spread out on mats to dry in the sun and raked over intermittently. In sunny weather, drying the beans usually takes about a week.

One of the toughest challenges of chocolate baking is to make a healthy birthday cake for children that they will enjoy, but won't send them into a sugar-induced spin. Here, instead of sweet icing and decorations, an imaginative use of fruit provides all the colour and shape you will need. Of course you can also add sweets and chocolate decorations once they are older – after all, what are birthdays for? Kids will also love creating a design – encourage them to come up with ideas for shapes and decoration.

FRUITY FISH

BIRTHDAY CAKE

Preparation time: 20 minutes
Baking time: 35 minutes, depending on the tin you use
Use: 31 x 27cm (12 x 11in) roasting tin or round cake tins
depending on the shape you need for your cake, large tray for serving
Serves: 15 (double the recipe and use two roasting tins if you want to make a cake
as large as the one in the photograph, which serves 30)

CAKE

12 eggs, separated

350g (12oz) sugar

200g (7oz) plain flour, sifted

100g (3$^1/_2$ oz) good-quality cocoa powder

175g (6oz) unsalted butter, melted and cooled

TOPPING SUGGESTIONS

Thick Greek yogurt mixed with a little honey or a smooth fruit compote are healthier alternatives to sugary icings.

Chocolate spread is another good quick, sticky topping for older children, but don't forget it includes hazelnuts!

100g (3$^1/_2$ oz) bars of chocolate melted with 1 tablespoon double cream per bar – try butterscotch chocolate for extra indulgence.

DECORATION

Quantities of different fruits of all colours and shapes. (Try slices of kiwi fruit for a cat's eyes, segments of orange or clementines for fish scales.)

Sweets, wafer fans, chocolate flakes, liquorice ropes, ice-cream cones, sticks of rock.

Toys and miniature figures.

Toothpicks and skewers are great for holding things together.

HINT: As you are making this cake at home and don't have to worry about transporting it, you can be as ambitious and extravagant as you please. Why not try three-dimensional designs?

To make the cake, preheat the oven to 180°C/350°F/gas mark 4. Line the baking tins with greaseproof paper.

Whisk the egg yolks with the sugar until thick and creamy. The mixture should be pale, and when you lift the whisk above the bowl it should fall from the whisk in a thick ribbon. Whisk the egg whites until light and fluffy. Sift the flour and the cocoa together and then fold in, in three or four stages, alternating with the egg whites and the melted, cooled butter.

Pour the mixture into the prepared tins and bake in the oven for about 35 minutes for a deep cake, about 20 minutes for a shallow one and 5–10 minutes if you are using a roasting tin. Once you begin to smell it cooking, take a look. To test whether the cake is done, insert a skewer into the centre and press the top of the cake. If the skewer comes out clean, and if the cake is springy and the edges have come away from the sides of the tin, it is done.

Leave the cake in the tin for a few minutes and then turn it out on to a wire rack to cool before removing the greaseproof paper.

To decorate, find a picture or figure of a character or scene to use as a guide. By studying it, you will find little details that will be easy to replicate using pieces of cake or fruit.

Prepare a large serving tray by covering it with foil or greaseproof paper.

Place the cake on a wooden board and, with a bread knife, cut it to your desired shape. You don't have to make the shape from one piece of cake, remember you can easily stick bits of cake together using the icing. Assemble your shape on the tray.

Ice the cake with your chosen topping, then let your imagination run wild. Try to group the same fruits together in blocks of colour to create a cake that children will adore.

Penny Parker gives heavenly teas and has many recipes that people are always asking for, which she is very happy to pass on. We are always surprised by the number of people who have sent us improvised recipes because their friend would not give them the original. These Chocolate Flapjacks are the original recipe and contain muscovado sugar, which gives them a rich flavour and takes the edge off the usual sweetness inherent in flapjacks.

CHOCOLATE
FLAPJACKS

Preparation time: 10 minutes
Baking time: 20 minutes
Use: 17 x 28cm (7 x 11in) baking tray or roasting tin
Makes: 20

350g (12oz) unsalted butter

3 tablespoons golden syrup

175g (6oz) soft brown sugar

175g (6oz) muscovado sugar

175g (6oz) good-quality oats (oat flakes)

275g (10oz) processed oats (rolled or porridge oats)

6 tablespoons good-quality cocoa powder

Preheat the oven to 140°C/275°F/gas mark 1. Butter the baking tray.

Melt the butter, syrup and both sugars in a saucepan. Do not allow to bubble. Mix in the oats and the cocoa.

Use a fork to press the mixture into the baking tray and bake for 18–20 minutes. The flapjacks need to cook to the centre but you don't want them to bubble, otherwise they will be too toffee-like. They should stay moist.

Remove from the oven and leave to cool for about 20 minutes before slicing up. Leave to cool completely before removing from the tray.

HINT: These flapjacks are delicious with 2 tablespoons of desiccated coconut, or
a handful of sultanas added with the oats. Equally tasty is 1 tablespoon of sesame seeds,
but you will also need a handful of extra oats because the seeds will make the flapjacks oily.

LICKING THE BOWL

Haley Foxen is the god-daughter of our founder, Josephine Fairley. Her mother was the chairman of the Soil Association and, together with Jo and Craig Sams, a driving force in the campaign for the return to farming methods that work in harmony with nature and that produce food with real taste. Haley gave us this recipe when Green & Black's was first launched.

CHOCOLATE
DIPPED FRUIT

Preparation time: 30 minutes
Use: wire rack or toothpicks and a block of polystyrene or two halves of a watermelon to support the dipped fruit
Makes: about 100 pieces

100g (3½ oz) milk chocolate, broken into pieces preferably 34% cocoa solids,

100g (3½ oz) good-quality white chocolate, broken into pieces

100g (3½ oz) Maya Gold, or a good-quality dark orange chocolate, broken into pieces

12 strawberries, stems in place

2 ripe kiwi fruit, sliced

12 cherries, stalks in place

1 pineapple, cut into triangular pieces

2 bananas, sliced at an angle

2 mangoes, sliced

1 punnet Cape gooseberries

2 dragon fruit, sliced into quarters, skin on

Melt the three chocolates separately in heatproof bowls suspended over a saucepan of barely simmering water. Take extra care with the white chocolate: you may want to melt it over a saucepan of boiled water off the heat. Leave to cool for about 5 minutes before dipping the fruit.

You can use toothpicks to skewer the prepared fruit, dipping the pieces so that each one is half-covered with chocolate, then stick them in the polystyrene or watermelon to set. Alternatively, hold the fruit with your fingers, dip in the chocolate and leave them to set on a wire rack. Continue until all the chocolate is used up.

Once dipped, do not put the fruit in the fridge otherwise the chocolate will lose its shine.

HINT: You can also freeze the prepared fruit before dunking it in the chocolate and then return it to the freezer on a tray lined with greaseproof paper for a sweltering, summer's day treat.

Why buy a processed muffin made with artificial flavours when they can be made so easily at home? These muffins are ideal for older children to make by themselves and can be eaten soon after they are removed from the oven.

BANANA, CHERRY AND WHITE CHOCOLATE

MUFFINS

Preparation time: 10 minutes
Cooking time: 20 minutes
Use: paper muffin cases or a 10-hole muffin tray
Makes: 10 large muffins

150g (5oz) plain flour

$\frac{1}{2}$ level tablespoon baking powder

$\frac{1}{4}$ teaspoon salt

1 medium egg

40g (1$\frac{1}{2}$oz) caster sugar

125ml (4fl oz) milk

50g (2oz) unsalted butter, melted

50g (2oz) dried cherries, chopped

50g (2oz) white chocolate, chopped

1 small banana, mashed

Preheat the oven to 200°C/400°F/gas mark 6.

Sift together the flour, baking powder and salt. In a separate bowl whisk together the egg, sugar, milk and melted butter. Mix the dry ingredients into the wet ingredients. Don't try to blend them too evenly because they should look a little lumpy. Add the cherries, white chocolate and mashed banana and stir, but again, do not overmix.

Spoon into the muffin cases or muffin tray, filling each approximately two-thirds full.

Bake for 20 minutes.

HINT: The muffin batter should not be evenly blended otherwise the muffins will have too smooth a texture and will be more like cup cakes.

The perfect after-supper pud served with fruit salad. Children love to do the flipping and watch the drop scones magically change their form. Ensure that they use giant oven gloves so that they don't get hit by any stray spits of fat, and make sure someone is there to hold the pan.

CHOCOLATE

DROP SCONES

Preparation time: 15 minutes
Cooking time: 20 minutes
Use: heavy-based frying pan and spatula
Makes: 18–20

100g (3½ oz) self-raising flour

1 teaspoon baking powder

3 tablespoons caster sugar

4 tablespoons cocoa powder

1 large egg

150ml (¼ pint) milk

100g (3½ oz) unsalted butter

Grated zest of 1 orange or
teaspoon grated fresh ginger (optional)

Sift the flour, baking powder, sugar and cocoa into a large bowl. Make a well in the centre and drop in the egg. Beat the egg, gradually drawing in the flour. Gradually add the milk a little at a time, slowly mixing the ingredients to form a smooth batter the consistency of thick pouring cream. Keep your actions gentle otherwise the drop scones will be tough.

Stir in one of the optional flavourings if you wish.

Melt the butter in the frying pan over a low heat and then pour it into a jug.

Test the temperature by cooking one drop scone first and then pour about a soupspoonful of the batter into the pan, cooking three drop scones at a time. Leave lots of space between them so that they don't join up.

Cook until a few bubbles appear on the surface and burst, then flip them, leaving them to cook on the other side for about 1 minute.

Add more melted butter to the pan between batches and ensure it covers the surface fully before cooking the next batch.

Serve immediately with butter, chocolate spread, sprinkled with sugar and a squeeze of lemon juice or jam and a dollop of cream.

HINT: To reheat, wrap in layers of aluminium foil and place in a warm oven for a few minutes.

CREATE A STIR

The dried beans must contain less than 7–8 per cent moisture,
which prevents mould growth during storage.

These will surprise you and only get better as you devour them and the heat of the chillies takes hold. Chilli is one of the oldest partners for chocolate and this is a great way to eat them and a wonderfully unusual teatime treat. Helen Garmston, one of the runners-up in our *Country Living* magazine recipe competition, first made these muffins as a dessert for a Mexican buffet supper. They are equally good for breakfast or brunch.

MEXICAN MOLE

MUFFINS

Preparation time: 15 minutes
Baking time: 20 minutes
Use: 12-hole muffin tin, 24 paper muffin cases
Makes: 12 muffins

100g (3^1/$_2$oz) milk chocolate, preferably 34% cocoa solids

10g (^{1}/$_2$oz) or more fresh red chillies (thumb- or finger-length chillies are likely to be medium hot)

200g (7oz) plain flour

25g (1oz) good-quality cocoa powder

1 teaspoon baking powder

^{1}/$_2$ teaspoon salt

110g (4oz) caster sugar

2 medium eggs

100ml (3^1/$_2$fl oz) sunflower oil

225g (8fl oz) milk

1 teaspoon vanilla extract

Preheat the oven to 200°C/400°F/gas mark 6. Line a 12-hole muffin tin with double muffin cases.

Coarsely grate the milk chocolate. Finely dice the red chillies, discarding the seeds and membrane, being careful not to touch the flesh of the chillies. It is best to use rubber gloves.

Sift the flour, cocoa, baking powder and salt into a bowl, and stir in the sugar, grated chocolate and diced chilli. Make a well in the centre.

In another bowl, beat the eggs and sunflower oil until foamy, then gradually beat in the milk and vanilla extract. Pour the dry ingredients into the well and stir until just combined. Don't be tempted to overmix, otherwise they will not have the rough texture of a traditional muffin.

Spoon the mixture into the paper cases, filling each three-quarters full. Bake for approximately 20 minutes, until the muffins are well-risen and springy.

Let the muffins cool in the tin for a few minutes and serve them warm, or turn them on to a wire rack to cool completely.

HINT: If you do touch the flesh of the chillies with your bare hands be extra careful not to touch your eyes.

The beetroot in this cake gives it a moist, velvety texture and just a hint of a purple colour. It is very beetrooty when you first eat it and then the flavour becomes less shocking as time goes by! Most cakes with vegetables in them were first made because of a surplus of home-grown vegetables. Vicki van Esch sent us this version, adapted from an Australian recipe.

CHOCOLATE

BEETROOT CAKE

Preparation time: 30 minutes
Cooking time: 50 minutes
Use: 18cm (7in) round cake tin
Makes: 8 slices

100g (3½ oz) drinking chocolate

230g (8oz) self-raising flour

200g (7oz) golden caster sugar

100g (3½ oz) dark chocolate,
minimum 60% cocoa solids, broken into pieces

125g (4½ oz) unsalted butter

250g (9oz) cooked beetroot

3 large eggs

TO SERVE

icing sugar for dusting

crème fraîche

Preheat the oven to 180°C/350°F/gas mark 4.

Butter and flour the cake tin.

Sift together the drinking chocolate and the self-raising flour, then mix in the sugar. Melt the chocolate and butter together in a heatproof bowl suspended over a saucepan of barely simmering water. Purée the beetroot in a food-processor, whisk the eggs, then stir them into the beetroot. Add the beetroot and the chocolate mixtures to the dry ingredients and mix together thoroughly.

Pour the mixture into the cake tin. Bake for 50 minutes or until a skewer inserted into the centre comes out clean. Remove from the oven and leave the cake to stand in its tin for 10 minutes before turning it out on to a wire rack to cool. Serve dusted with icing sugar and some crème fraîche.

HINT: To give the cake a dramatic topping you could grate some cooked beetroot and add it to a standard white icing. Remember to use rubber gloves when handling the beetroot – it stains the skin!

Delicate hands are needed for this hedonistic pudding sent to us by Phillip Harris-Jones, who grows his own chillies. Late one night towards the end of a dinner party, he served thinly sliced chillies that had been marinating in vodka with a bar of Green & Black's Dark Chocolate; one thing led to another and his next dinner-party guests enjoyed these unforgettable chocolates.

VODKA CHILLI
CHOCOLATES

Marinating time: 12 hours
Preparation time: 30 minutes
Use: piping bag and small nozzle
Makes: 12 chilli chocolates

6 green chilli peppers, stalks on

6 red chilli peppers, stalks on

350ml (12fl oz) vodka

100g (3½ oz) good-quality white chocolate or dark chocolate, minimum 60% cocoa solids to fill the chillies

black pepper, freshly ground

100g (3½ oz) dark chocolate, minimum 60% cocoa solids

icing sugar

Wash the chillies, then cut a small slit in the side of each one to allow you to remove the inner membrane and all the seeds, so they are ready to be filled. Marinate the prepared chillies in the vodka for at least 12 hours before you prepare the filling.

To make the filling, melt the white or dark chocolate in a heatproof bowl suspended over a saucepan of barely simmering water. Remove from the heat and mix in a shot of vodka and some freshly ground pepper. Fill the chillies using a piping bag fitted with a small nozzle, or, if you don't have one, use a coffee spoon and a chopstick instead. Store the chillies in a container in the freezer until needed.

Sift icing sugar over a serving plate. Grind some black pepper over the icing sugar.

To dip the chillies, melt the dark chocolate in a heatproof bowl suspended over a saucepan of barely simmering water. Pour the melted chocolate into a glass and dip the chillies so that they are three-quarters coated in chocolate. Place them directly on to the serving plate to set before serving.

HINT: It is possible to blanch the de-seeded chillies to soften their flavour or boil them for 2 minutes to remove most of their heat.

You don't need a sausage machine to make these heavenly sausages, but you will need a butcher who can sell you some organic pork sausage casings. Zena Leech-Calton entered our National Trust competition and this recipe leapt out at us as we trawled through all the entries. Testing and tasting the sausages was an adventure, but filling the sausage casings manually proved to be much easier than we had imagined it would be.

SPICY ORGANIC PORK & HERB
CHILEAN CHOCOLATE SAUSAGES

Preparation time: 30 minutes
Resting time: overnight
Cooking: 10–15 minutes
Makes: 16 small sausages or 10 large ones
Use: sausage machine or large piping bag, 2–3cm ($^3/_4$–1in) nozzle

enough sausage casings for 1kg ($2^1/_4$ lb) mix

1 tablespoon vinegar

500g (18oz) organic belly of pork, coarsely minced

250g (9oz) organic belly of pork, diced small

2 sage leaves, chopped

1 teaspoon chopped coriander leaves and stalks

1 teaspoon chopped flat leaf parsley leaves

1 teaspoon chopped lemon thyme

25g (1oz) unsalted butter

1 tablespoon corn oil

175g (6oz) red onion, finely chopped

1 green chilli, de-seeded and finely chopped

10g ($^1/_2$ in) root ginger, peeled and finely chopped

2 garlic cloves, crushed

$^1/_2$ teaspoon ground mace

$^1/_2$ teaspoon ground paprika

$^1/_4$ teaspoon freshly grated nutmeg

$^1/_4$ teaspoon ground cumin

90g ($3^1/_4$ oz) dark chocolate, minimum 60% cocoa solids, broken into pieces

salt and freshly ground black pepper

Soak the sausage casings in a bowl of tepid water with a tablespoon of vinegar for 30 minutes. They will become soft and elastic. Wash the casings thoroughly in cold water then run water through them by attaching them to the tap.

Mix the minced and diced pork, sage, coriander, parsley and lemon thyme in a bowl using your hands.

Heat the butter and oil in a frying pan and sauté the red onion, chilli pepper, ginger and garlic until soft, but not browned. Add the mace, paprika, nutmeg and cumin to the sautéed mixture while it is still hot. Cook together for a few minutes to release the flavour of the spices.

Melt the chocolate in a heatproof bowl, suspended over a saucepan of barely simmering water.

Add the onion and spice mixture and the melted chocolate to the bowl of pork and mix together well, seasoning with a good dash of salt and pepper.

Cover the bowl and leave in the fridge overnight.

Load up your sausage machine or piping bag with the filling (if using a piping bag do not put all the filling into the piping bag at once as it makes it more difficult to force it through). Ease the casing over the nozzle, tying the casing at the end and leaving about 7cm (3in) hanging loose. Feed the filling through to make one long, fat sausage, then once the casing is almost full, tie a knot at the top end. Divide it into individual sausages by twisting each section in alternate directions to prevent the sausages unwinding. Cut the sausages in the middle of each twisted section.

Blanch the sausages in boiling, salted water for 1 minute before grilling or barbecuing them. Turn them frequently and try not to overcook them.

These sausages are delicious served with steamed brown rice flavoured with ginger and a two-bean salsa salad made with black beans, cannellini beans, olive oil, tomatoes, avocados, coriander, garlic, peppers, onions and seasoning.

TREASURES

Traces of caffeine and theobromine were discovered in 2002 in the remains of a brew found in cooking pots in northern Belize. The pots came from a Maya burial site *c.*600BC and showed that chocolate was used for food 1,000 years earlier than previously thought and that it was the Maya, not the Aztecs, who were the first to make a drink from it.

Martine Hilton's mother grew up on the plantations of Sumatra and Java surrounded by cacao pods. Her father, who had trained as a chemist, devised a method of roasting the beans and then hand-grinding them to make bars of rich, fatty chocolate. This is a family recipe based upon ingredients that were available to her grandparents such as fresh coconut, tins of condensed milk and her grandmother's favourite, hot ginger. Martine says it was often served when the ladies changed from sarongs into sweltering European dress after lunch to receive visitors. She has adapted this recipe and serves these squares at Christmas with Javanese coffee.

JAVANESE

GINGER SQUARES

Preparation time: 15 minutes
Chilling time: overnight
Use: 17 x 28cm (7 x 11in) baking tray
Makes: about 25

400g (14oz) dark chocolate, minimum 60% cocoa solids, broken into pieces

125g (4¹/₂ oz) unsalted butter

425g (15oz) or 425ml (15fl oz) tinned condensed milk

250g (9oz) Gingernut biscuits

250g (9oz) crystallised ginger

75g (3oz) flaked coconut

Melt the chocolate in a heatproof bowl suspended over a saucepan of barely simmering water. Stir in the butter and condensed milk.

Crush the biscuits roughly in a plastic bag with a rolling pin. Chop the ginger into small pieces and set about a quarter aside. Stir the biscuits, the remaining ginger and the coconut into the chocolate mixture.

Spoon the mixture into the tin lined with greaseproof paper and level the surface. Dot the surface with the reserved pieces of ginger.

Chill overnight before lifting out, using the paper, and cutting into small squares.

HINT: Flaked coconut can be found in health shops and specialist food stores.

Florentines are another of those tempting treats that one eyes in pâtisserie windows, never imagining they could be within reach of the home cook. They are, in fact, not nearly as complicated as they look.

FLORENTINES

Preparation time: 20 minutes
Cooking time: 10–12 minutes
Cooling and decorating time: 25 minutes
Use: 7cm (2³/₄in) biscuit cutter, 2 baking sheets, preferably non-stick with little bumps
Makes: about 24

50g (2oz) unsalted butter

125ml (4fl oz) double cream

125g (4¹/₂ oz) sugar

40g (1¹/₂ oz) glacé cherries, rinsed in hot water, drained, and cut into quarters

150g (5oz) blanched almonds, finely chopped

50g (2oz) slivered almonds

100g (3¹/₂ oz) candied orange peel, finely chopped

50g (2oz) plain flour

250g (9oz) dark chocolate,
minimum 60% cocoa solids, broken into pieces

Preheat the oven to 180°C/350°F/gas mark 4. Butter and lightly flour the baking sheets.

Melt the butter with the cream and sugar and bring slowly to the boil. Remove from the heat and stir in the cherries, the chopped and slivered almonds and the candied peel, and sift in the flour.

Drop a teaspoonful of the mixture on to the baking sheets, spacing well apart, and flatten each one with a fork dipped in cold water. They will double in size as they cook.

Bake for 5–6 minutes, remove from the oven and coax them into a circular shape by placing the biscuit cutter over it. Return to the oven and bake for a further 5–6 minutes until lightly browned at the edges. Remove from the oven and leave to set for a few minutes on the baking sheets, then use a palette knife to transfer them to a rack to cool.

Melt the chocolate in a heatproof bowl suspended over a saucepan of barely simmering water. Spread the smooth undersides of the florentines with chocolate using a palette knife. When it is on the point of setting create wavy lines across the chocolate by dragging a serrated knife from side to side across the chocolate. Leave to set.

HINT: This recipe is also delicious using milk, white or Maya Gold Chocolate.

A brazil nut has the calorie content of half an egg and is especially rich in amino acids so you may feel a mixture of guilt and contentment as you tuck into these delicious biscuits. This recipe was sent to us by Lorna Dowell, another of our National Trust chocolate competition finalists. Lorna was inspired to experiment after a delicious tea at the National Trust site at Dapdune Wharf where she ate soft-baked chocolate chip biscuits.

CHOCOLATE BRAZIL

SOFT-BAKED BISCUITS

Preparation time: 15 minutes
Cooking time: 20 minutes
Use: 6.5cm (2¹/₂in) biscuit cutter
Makes: 20

75g (3oz) unsalted butter

60g (2¹/₂ oz) caster sugar

1 large egg, beaten

175g (6oz) wholemeal self-raising flour

¹/₂ teaspoon vanilla extract

1–2 tablespoons milk

75g (3oz) dark chocolate,
minimum 60% cocoa solids, roughly chopped

75g (3oz) milk chocolate,
preferably 34% cocoa solids, roughly chopped

50g (2oz) brazil nuts, chopped

pinch of salt

Preheat the oven to 180°C/350°F/gas mark 4. Grease a baking sheet with melted butter.

Cream together the butter and sugar in a bowl until light and fluffy. Beat in the egg. Sift the flour once, returning the bran from the wholemeal flour that has remained in the sieve to the sifted flour, then fold it into the mixture. The bran gives a distinctive flavour and texture to the biscuits. Beat well, adding the vanilla extract and sufficient milk to make a pliable dough. Mix it with your hands, adding the milk in stages until the dough is fairly soft, but not sticky. Add the chopped chocolate, nuts and salt and distribute evenly through the dough. Roll out on to a lightly floured board to a thickness of about 5mm (¹/₄in). Stamp into rounds and place the biscuits, spaced well apart, on the greased baking sheet.

Bake in the centre of the oven for about 20 minutes. Watch them carefully so they don't overcook. Remove from the oven and leave to cool on the baking tray for a few minutes before transferring to a wire rack to cool completely.

HINT: All flour should be sifted before you use it. Sifting flour is important, not just to remove any little foreign bodies that may be in the flour, but also to aerate it.

Gingerbread was made with spices, ginger and honey in medieval times, but in the seventeenth century, the honey was replaced by treacle. Teresa Jackson makes this chocolate recipe for the Halloween Carnival that takes place in Belfast each year. She has been spreading the word about real chocolate and Fairtrade at work and has been a great fan of Green & Black's for many years.

CHOCOLATE SPICE
GINGERBREAD

Preparation time: 40 minutes
Cooking time: 50 minutes
Use: 18cm (7in) square cake tin, 7.5cm (3in) deep
Makes: 8 slices

125g (4¹/₂ oz) unsalted butter

50g (2oz) Maya Gold or other good-quality dark orange chocolate, broken into pieces

50g (2oz) dark chocolate, minimum 60% cocoa solids, broken into pieces

75g (3oz) dark muscovado sugar

4 tablespoons treacle

150ml (¹/₄ pint) buttermilk

125g (4¹/₂ oz) ready-to-eat prunes

175g (6oz) plain flour

1 teaspoon bicarbonate of soda

2 level teaspoons ground ginger

1 level teaspoon cinnamon

1 large egg, lightly beaten

Preheat the oven to 160°C/325°F/gas mark 3. Line the tin with greaseproof paper or baking parchment.

Cut the butter into cubes and place in a heavy saucepan along with the chocolate, sugar, treacle and buttermilk. Heat gently until the ingredients have melted, then set aside to cool.

Snip the prunes into small pieces with kitchen scissors. Sift the flour into a large bowl along with the bicarbonate of soda and spices. Pour the chocolate mixture into the bowl and beat thoroughly with a wooden spoon, then add the beaten egg and beat again. Fold in the prunes.

Pour the mixture into the prepared tin and level off the surface using a palette knife. Bake for about 50 minutes. Remove from the oven and leave to cool in the tin for about 10 minutes. Turn out on to a wire rack and leave to cool completely. Wrap in grease-proof paper and store in an airtight container.

HINT: This cake is wonderfully moist and will keep for a week in an airtight container. It is best eaten the day after it is made.

Dr Barry Alcock, a runner-up in our National Trust Chocolate Recipe Competition, sent us this regional French recipe which originates in St Pourçain on the upper Loire. He points out that 'these feather-light cakes have a name for which there is no polite translation. They are simply "Nun's Farts".'

PETS

DE NONNE

Preparation time: 20 minutes
Cooking time: 4 hours or overnight
Makes: 50
Use: 2 non-stick baking sheets

150g (5oz) dark chocolate,
minimum 60% cocoa solids, roughly chopped

3 large egg whites

salt

125g (4½ oz) caster sugar

125g (4½ oz) walnuts, roughly chopped

25g (1oz) angelica, diced

2 teaspoons dark rum

Preheat the oven to 180°C/350°F/gas mark 4. If you don't have non-stick baking sheets, line ordinary ones with foil.

Place the roughly chopped chocolate in the fridge for about 1 hour.

Whisk the egg whites with a pinch of salt until stiff peaks form. Whisk in the sugar a little at a time until the mixture becomes glossy. Fold in the nuts, chocolate and angelica and then fold in the rum.

Place heaped teaspoons of the mixture, spaced well apart, on the baking sheets.

Bake in the oven for 5 minutes and then turn off the oven and leave them for about 4 hours or overnight.

Store the cakes in an airtight container.

HINT: Be careful not to overbeat the egg whites. They should form stiff, shiny peaks, but if they start to separate and resemble snow, you have gone too far.

Roger Moore sent in this recipe with a note saying 'My late mother-in-law was an accomplished cook, whose cakes and puddings were irresistible to potential sons-in-law. The origins of her recipes lay in a motley collection of old, well-thumbed cookery books, though most had been adapted using the personal touch, as they became family traditions. The Chocolate Apple Cake has always been my favourite and seems to improve over time, if any is left over for tomorrow!'

MY MOTHER-IN-LAW'S

CHOCOLATE APPLE CAKE

Preparation time: 30 minutes
Cooking time: 50–55 minutes
Use: 21cm (8¹/₂in) sandwich tin
Serves: 8

CAKE

140g (4³/₄oz) hazelnuts

275g (10oz) unsalted butter

175g (6oz) caster sugar

3 large eggs

275g (10oz) self-raising flour

1 teaspoon baking powder

4 tablespoons strong coffee

50g (2oz) dark chocolate,
minimum 60% cocoa solids, coarsely grated

FILLING

700g (1¹/₂lb) Bramley apples

1 large lemon

2 dessertspoons rhubarb jam or fruit compôte

ICING

200g (7oz) dark chocolate,
minimum 60% cocoa solids, broken into pieces

25g (1oz) unsalted butter

2 drops vanilla extract

1 teaspoon strong coffee

Preheat the oven to 180°C/350°F/gas mark 4. Butter and flour the sandwich tin.

To make the cake, crush the hazelnuts, not too finely, and grill lightly until they are golden. They burn very easily so keep a close eye on them. Cream the butter and sugar together. Whisk the eggs and add to the creamed mixture with a little flour. Mix together well. Sift in the remainder of the flour and the baking powder and enough coffee to make a soft mix. Set aside 25g (1oz) of the grilled hazelnuts, then fold in the remainder into the mixture, along with the coarsely grated chocolate.

Pour the mixture into the sandwich tin. Bake for 50–55 minutes. Leave the cake to cool a little in the tin, before turning out to cool completely on a wire rack.

Meanwhile, prepare the filling. Peel and roughly chop the Bramley apples. Place in a saucepan with the grated rind and juice of the lemon and the jam. Cover and cook on a low heat, stirring occasionally, until the apple pieces are soft, but not mushy.

Once the cake has cooled, carefully cut it in half and fill with the cooled apple.

To make the icing, melt the chocolate with the coffee in a heatproof bowl suspended over a saucepan of barely simmering water. Remove from the heat and stir in the butter and vanilla extract. Leave to cool a little before pouring over the cake, allowing the icing to run gently over the sides.

Decorate with the reserved hazelnuts.

HINT: This cake can be made with almost any nuts, especially pine nuts or almonds, which do not have to be grilled.

Once they arrive at the chocolate factory, the beans are de-stoned and cleaned. A brief, intense blast of heat is fired at them to loosen the shells from the nibs that nestle inside. Crushers, sieves and streams of air are then used to force open the shells and release the nibs.

Philippa Jacobs lived in Cape Town for three years and this is her favourite South African recipe. It always reminds her of the very wet Cape winters when a walk with her dogs on the slopes of Table Mountain in the rain and wind was followed by a traditional Sunday roast and Tipsy Tart. Her variation on the recipe includes a covering of grated dark chocolate.

CAPE GINGER
TIPSY TART

Preparation time: 40 minutes
Baking time: 35 minutes
Use: 23cm (9in) flan or pie dish size suitable for serving

BATTER

1 teaspoon bicarbonate of soda

240g (8½ oz) dates, stoned
(or 250g/8oz box with stones), chopped

125ml (4fl oz) boiling water

40g (1½ oz) unsalted butter

200g (7oz) granulated sugar

2 large eggs

250g (9oz) plain flour

1 teaspoon baking powder

pinch of salt

25g (1oz) preserved ginger, chopped

100g (3½ oz) glacé or dried cherries, chopped

40g (1½ oz) walnuts, chopped

50g (2oz) dark chocolate,
minimum 60% cocoa solids

SYRUP

75g (3oz) granulated sugar

200ml (7fl oz) water

salt

1 teaspoon vanilla extract

25g (1oz) unsalted butter

60ml (2fl oz) brandy or dark rum

double cream or vanilla ice cream to serve

Preheat the oven to 180°C/350°F/gas mark 4. Grease the dish well with butter.

Pat the bicarbonate of soda on to the dates and pour the boiling water over them, stir and leave to cool.

Cream the butter and sugar, add the eggs and beat thoroughly. Sift together the flour, baking powder and salt and stir into the creamed mixture.

Add the date mixture, ginger, cherries and walnuts.

Spoon the mixture into the pie dish and bake for 35 minutes. Place the chocolate in the freezer.

Prepare the syrup so you can pour it over the tart the minute it comes out of the oven.

Boil all the ingredients for the syrup together for about 6 minutes until they form a syrup.

Remove the tart from the oven and prick the surface all over with a fork. Immediately pour over the hot syrup, then grate the chilled chocolate over the top before serving with a dollop of cream.

HINT: If you prefer, you can use pecan nuts instead of walnuts.

Strictly, these aren't really tuiles as the original golden 'tuiles' are named after the tiles that dominate the rooftops of Provence. These Chocolate Tuiles still bear the curved shape, but their colour has changed. They are the perfect accompaniment to ice cream or a chocolate mousse.

CHOCOLATE

TUILES

Preparation time: 10 minutes
Chilling time: 1 hour
Cooking time: 15 minutes
Use: non-stick baking sheet, preferably one with little round bumps all over it
Makes: 12

1 large egg

1 large egg white

125g (4½ oz) icing sugar

25g (1oz) plain flour

10g (½ oz) cocoa powder

1 teaspoon double cream

25g (1oz) unsalted butter, melted and cooled

125g (4½ oz) pine nuts and slivered hazelnuts

Whisk together the egg and the egg white in a bowl. Add the icing sugar, flour, cocoa, cream and melted butter in that order and mix until smooth. Stir in the pine nuts and slivered hazelnuts.

Place heaped tablespoons of the mixture on to the non-stick trays, ensuring they are spaced well apart, and refrigerate for 1 hour.

Preheat the oven to 180°C/350°F/gas mark 4.

Dip a fork in warm water and, shaking off any excess water, flatten the mixture into discs using the back of the fork.

Bake for 10 minutes or until the 'tuiles' are firm and have an even colour. Remove from the oven and immediately place them over a rolling pin to give them a curved shape. Leave to cool and store in an airtight container.

HINT: The 'tuiles' look wonderful served upside down, overlapping one another in rows in the same way as they would be laid on a roof in the south of France.

If you need to make this recipe for more than six people double the quantities but use two separate tins – it begins to look like a great beast if you make one enormous one! This healthier version of a meringue roulade which uses yogurt instead of cream is delicious with almost any fruit but looks especially effective if you use green and red grapes or any berries.

MERINGUE ROULADE
WITH CHOCOLATE

Preparation time: 30 minutes
Cooking time: 45 minutes
Use: 38 x 28cm (15 x 11in) baking tray
Serves: 6–8

ROULADE

4 large egg whites

225g (8oz) caster sugar

2–3 tablespoons icing sugar for dusting

2 tablespoons cocoa powder for dusting

500ml (18fl oz) full-fat Greek-style yogurt

100g (3½oz) dark chocolate, minimum 60% cocoa solids, chopped into small chunks

310g (11oz) raspberries

RASPBERRY COULIS

225g (8oz) raspberries

45g (1½oz) icing sugar

Cut out two sheets of greaseproof paper or baking parchment so that the sides rise about 5cm (2in) above the base of the baking tray. Butter and then line the baking sheet with one piece of the parchment. Reserve the other piece.

Preheat the oven to 100°C/200°F/gas mark 0.

Whisk the egg whites until soft peaks form. Continue to whisk, gradually adding half the sugar. Continue to whisk until the mixture is stiff but not dry. Fold in the remainder of the sugar.

Spoon the meringue into the prepared paper case, spreading it evenly into the corners. Bake in the preheated oven for 40–45 minutes until it is lightly coloured and firm yet spongy when pressed. Leave to cool for about 1 hour.

To make the coulis, purée the raspberries in a blender and then pass them through a sieve into a bowl. Stir in the icing sugar to taste.

Place a large sheet of greaseproof paper or baking parchment on the work surface and dust with the icing sugar and the cocoa powder. Turn the baked meringue (still in its paper) upside down on to the large sheet so that what was the top of the meringue is now on the icing sugar and cocoa, and is the bottom. Carefully peel away the paper.

Spread the yogurt over the meringue. Scatter the chocolate chunks evenly over the yogurt base and then scatter the raspberries on to the layer of chocolate chunks. Very carefully roll up the roulade using the paper as a support. Reserve any remaining icing sugar and cocoa to sprinkle over the roulade before serving. Chill in the fridge until required, but for no more than 5 hours. Serve with the raspberry coulis.

HINT: Do not worry about the meringue cracking slightly as you roll it up as it will look beautiful once you have sprinkled the reserved icing sugar and cocoa over it.

Jo Gilks gave up her lucrative job in the City of London for food. She has always loved to cook and has forged a very different, yet often equally stressful, career for herself as a chef. Her Chocolate Pecan Pie has become a Thanksgiving dinner favourite and she warns you not to be put off by the crumbly texture of the pastry – it is difficult to roll but worth the trouble.

JO'S CHOCOLATE

PECAN PIE

Preparation time: 35 minutes plus 25 minutes chilling
Cooking time: 1 hour 25 minutes
Use: 28cm (11in) loose-based tart tin
Serves 8–10

PASTRY

275g (10oz) plain flour

75g (3oz) icing sugar

150g (5oz) unsalted butter, cold

2 large egg yolks

FILLING

275g (10oz) dark chocolate,
minimum 60% cocoa solids, broken into pieces

200g (7oz) shelled pecans, chopped

3 large eggs, beaten

225g (8oz) light soft brown sugar

250ml (9fl oz) evaporated milk

1 teaspoon vanilla extract

50g (2oz) unsalted butter, melted

To make the pastry, sift together the flour and icing sugar and cut the butter into cubes.

Place in a food-processor and mix together, adding the egg yolks at the end to form a dough.

Carefully roll out the pastry. You will need quite a lot of flour on your board and rolling pin as it sticks easily. The pastry needs to be very thin. Lift it carefully into the tart tin by rolling it up on the rolling pin, then slowly unroll it over the tin, press into the base and sides and trim away the excess, but allow a little extra as the pastry will shrink slightly. Chill in the fridge for about 30 minutes. Preheat the oven to 180°C/350°F/gas mark 4.

Bake the pastry case blind by using parchment or greaseproof paper and baking beans for about 15 minutes.

Remove the beans and paper and return the pastry to the oven for a further 10 minutes or until it has developed a very light colour. Remove from the oven and set aside while you make the filling. Reduce the oven temperature to 160°C/325°F/gas mark 3.

Melt the chocolate in a heatproof bowl suspended over a saucepan of barely simmering water. Mix together all the remaining ingredients for the filling, then stir in the melted chocolate. Spoon into the pastry case and return it to the oven for about 1 hour. Watch the pastry carefully and if necessary cover with foil to prevent it burning.

HINT: Any dried beans or pulses can be used for blind baking – red, kidney, black, corn or rice – all they are doing is putting weight on the pastry so that it doesn't rise during baking. Once cooled, they can be used again and again.

MYSTICAL

Hurricane Iris devastated Belize on 21 October 2001. It destroyed many homes and crops and caused havoc for the cacao that survived, but more cacao trees have since been replanted by the growers. This cacao pod has been bored into by a woodpecker.

The drama of a soufflé straight from the oven will always stir a table of dinner-party guests. Remember the success of a soufflé is in the rising so take note of the hints at the bottom of the page. This is another of our trusted tester Jo Gilks's foolproof recipes.

CHOCOLATE SOUFFLÉ
WITH BUTTERSCOTCH SAUCE

Preparation time: 20 minutes
Cooking time: 10-15 minutes
Use: 6 x 6cm (2¹/₂ in) ramekins
Serves: 6

1 teaspoon unsalted butter

1 tablespoon caster sugar

1 tablespoon cocoa powder

SOUFFLE

100g (4oz) dark chocolate,
minimum 60% cocoa solids, broken into pieces

60g (2¹/₂ oz) cocoa powder

8 egg whites

60g (2¹/₂ oz) caster sugar

BUTTERSCOTCH SAUCE

100g (3¹/₂ oz) butterscotch chocolate,
broken into pieces

4 tablespoons milk

Preheat the oven to 190°C/375°F/gas mark 5.

To prepare the ramekins, melt the butter and brush the insides of the ramekins. Mix the sugar with the cocoa and sprinkle into each ramekin until coated, shaking out any excess. Set aside.

Melt the chocolate in a heatproof bowl suspended over a saucepan of barely simmering water.

Mix the cocoa with 150ml (¹/₄ pint) of cold water in a saucepan then bring to the boil whisking continuously. Boil for 10 seconds. Transfer the cocoa mixture to a mixing bowl and mix with the melted chocolate.

Prepare the Butterscotch Sauce so that it will be ready when you serve the soufflé. Melt the chocolate with the milk in a small saucepan over a very low heat until the chocolate and butterscotch pieces are melted and combined with the milk. Stir before serving.

Continue with the soufflés by whisking the egg whites until soft peaks form. Add the sugar and continue whisking until stiff peaks form. Add one-quarter of the egg white to the cocoa mixture and whisk until thoroughly blended. Gently fold in the remaining egg white using a metal spoon to cut through the egg white as you fold so that you do not knock the air out of it.

Fill each prepared ramekin to the rim with the soufflé mixture and, using a palette knife, level off the surface. Run your thumb around the rim of each ramekin, pushing away the soufflé mixture, so that it does not stick to the edge and will rise evenly.

Bake the soufflés for about 10–15 minutes. Remove from the oven and pour a little Butterscotch Sauce over each soufflé and serve immediately.

HINT: When brushing the ramekins with the melted butter, brush from the base of the ramekin up towards the rim – this seems to help the soufflé to rise evenly. Remember not to open the oven door while the soufflé is cooking or the rush of cold air may prevent it from rising as high as you would wish.

Not such a predictable pudding after all, each of these mousses is a little different from the next one — sometimes it's the texture and with others a surprise flavour. Only the Chocolate and Lemongrass Mousse will take more than 25 minutes to prepare and at the most they will take 6 hours to set.

EGGLESS
HILARY METH'S

Chill for a minimum of 2 hours. Serves 4–6

200g (7oz) dark chocolate,
minimum 60% cocoa solids, broken into pieces

400ml (14fl oz) coconut milk, tinned

2 gelatine leaves

2 level tablespoons icing sugar

2 teaspoons vanilla extract

Melt the chocolate in a heatproof bowl suspended over a saucepan of barely simmering water. Gently heat the coconut milk, add the gelatine leaves and stir until they have dissolved. Sift the icing sugar and add to the coconut milk, stirring to dissolve. Finally, add the vanilla essence and the melted chocolate and whisk together. Dust with cocoa and decorate with roasted coffee beans, coconut flakes or toasted pine nuts.

LIGHT
AND DARK

Chill for a minimum of 1 hour. Serves 6

200g (7oz) dark chocolate,
minimum 60% cocoa solids, finely chopped

50ml (2fl oz) full-cream milk

2 large egg yolks

$\frac{1}{2}$ teaspoon vanilla extract

4 large egg whites

40g (1$\frac{1}{2}$oz) caster sugar

Melt the chocolate and the milk in a heatproof bowl suspended over a saucepan of barely simmering water. Stir together and then set aside to cool slightly. Stir the egg yolks into the chocolate until well blended, then stir in the vanilla extract. Whisk the egg whites until soft peaks form. Add the sugar gradually and continue to whisk until stiff and glossy. Stir a ladleful of egg whites into the chocolate mixture to lighten it, then gently fold in the rest of the egg whites. Transfer the mixture into your chosen container and chill for at least an hour.

HINT: Always use eggs at room temperature. Do not overwhisk egg whites and remember to use a clean bowl. Use the melted chocolate while it is still warm to the touch. Do not allow the melted chocolate and egg yolk mixture to cool down too much, otherwise it will be difficult to mix in the egg whites.

WHITE CHOCOLATE, CARDAMOM MOUSSE

NIGEL SLATER'S

Chill for 4 hours. Serves 6–8

8 plump green cardamom pods

100ml (3½ fl oz) milk

3 bay leaves

250g (9oz) good-quality white chocolate, broken into pieces

300ml (½ pint) double cream

3 large egg whites

cocoa powder for dusting

Crack open the cardamom pods and extract the seeds. Crush them lightly and then put them with the milk and the bay leaves in a small saucepan. Gently warm the milk until it is close to boiling point, then remove from the heat and set aside to infuse. Melt the chocolate in a heatproof bowl suspended over a saucepan of barely simmering water. As soon as it starts to melt turn off the heat, leaving the bowl in place. Whip the cream to form soft mounds; it should not be stiff. Whisk the egg whites until stiff peaks form. Once the chocolate has melted, remove from the heat and sieve the warm milk mixture into it. Mix the chocolate and milk together until velvety. Stir in a spoonful of the egg whites to the chocolate mixture, then gently fold in the remaining egg whites using a large metal spoon. Gently fold in the softly whipped cream. Spoon into containers and refrigerate for 4 hours. Dust with cocoa just before serving.

DARK

WITH COFFEE

Chill for at least 6 hours. Serves 6

150g (5oz) dark chocolate,
minimum 60% cocoa solids, broken into pieces

2 tablespoons filter coffee

60g (2½ oz) unsalted butter

3 large eggs, separated

3 tablespoons caster sugar

Cocoa powder

Melt the chocolate with the coffee and the butter in a heatproof bowl suspended over a saucepan of barely simmering water. Remove from the heat and stir. Stir in the egg yolks until the mixture is very smooth. Whisk the egg whites until soft peaks form, add the sugar and whisk until the mixture is stiff and glossy. Fold a ladleful into the chocolate and then add the rest of the egg whites delicately, to retain as much air as possible and ensuring no white spots from the meringue remain. Spoon into a serving bowl or six individual ramekins and chill for at least 6 hours. Dust with cocoa powder before serving but do not return the mousse to the fridge at this stage as the cocoa will absorb moisture.

A French family gave Angela Dempsey this recipe in the Seventies. She has since added the blackcurrants and honey which has confirmed its position as her family's favourite pudding.

BITTER CHOCOLATE MOUSSE
WITH BLACKCURRANTS

Chill for a minimum of 1 hour. Serves 4–6

4 tablespoons of blackcurrants topped and tailed or tinned blackcurrants, strained

1 dessertspoon clear honey

150g (5oz) Hazelnut and Currant Dark Chocolate or other good-quality fruit and nut chocolate

5 egg whites

25g (1oz) caster sugar

2 egg yolks

Gently stew the blackcurrants in the honey. Once softened, remove from the heat and leave to cool. Melt the chocolate in a heatproof bowl suspended over a saucepan of barely simmering water and leave to cool slightly. Whisk the egg whites until soft peaks form, then add the sugar. Continue to beat until stiff and glossy. Stir the egg yolks into the melted chocolate then mix in one-third of the egg whites. Gently fold in the remainder of the egg whites. Spoon the blackcurrants into the base of your containers, then pour in the chocolate mousse. Chill for at least 1 hour before serving.

SIMPLE WHITE

Chill for a minimum of 4 hours. Serves 4–6

400g (14oz) good-quality white chocolate, broken into pieces

3 gelatine leaves

700ml (1¼ pints) whipping cream

5 large egg yolks

125g (4½ oz) icing sugar

3–4 tablespoons Grand Marnier

Melt the chocolate in a heatproof bowl suspended over a saucepan of barely simmering water. Dissolve the gelatine in two tablespoons of warmed cream. Beat the egg yolks and sugar, add the Grand Marnier, gelatine cream and melted chocolate, and stir together well. Whip the remainder of the cream until thick and then fold into the chocolate and egg yolk mixture. Pour into a mould or individual ramekins and chill for 4 hours. This mousse is delicious served with a raspberry coulis and visitandines or with a crust of melted dark chocolate, poured over and left to harden.

HINT: Remember to use a metal spoon when folding in the egg whites and to cut through the mixture as you fold. This way you do not knock the air out of the egg whites and the mousse remains light and fluffy.

Rachel Green runs her own business cooking for four to four hundred people. She has cooked many times for the Royal Family and was recently filmed by the BBC. It was at a demonstration in aid of the Bosnian Support Fund, a charity that supports the continuing needs of refugees in Bosnia, that we tried this recipe. A farmer's daughter from Lincolnshire, Rachel is dedicated to supporting and promoting regional producers.

CHOCOLATE AND LEMONGRASS

MOUSSE

Chilling time: 2 hours
Serves: 6

3 sticks of lemongrass

200ml (7fl oz) milk

270g (10 oz) milk chocolate,
preferably 34% cocoa solids, broken into pieces

1$^{1}/_{2}$ gelatine leaves

50g (2oz) caster sugar

300ml ($^{1}/_{2}$ pint) double cream

Finely chop the lemongrass into small pieces or grind in a food-processor or pestle and mortar. Pour the milk into a large, heavy-based saucepan, add the lemongrass and bring to the boil. Remove from the heat and leave to infuse for 1 hour. Melt the chocolate in a heatproof bowl suspended over a saucepan of barely simmering water. Whisk the sugar and gelatine into the milk and return to a low heat, stirring continuously until the gelatine has melted. Remove from the heat and stir in the melted chocolate. Leave to cool slightly. Pass the mixture through a sieve to remove the lemongrass. Allow to cool down completely. Whip the cream in a bowl until it begins to thicken, but it should not be too stiff. Gently fold into the chocolate mixture. Spoon the mousse into your chosen containers.

HINT: Set the mousse first in a large bowl before transferring to individual containers, then using a tablespoon and a clean finger, you can mould the mousse into your desired shape before garnishing.

This is one of those recipes that people either love or hate. It is irresistible if you are addicted to Toblerone or like a sweet mousse and is the ultimate test of whether you have a sweet tooth.

CHOCOLATE NOUGAT
MOUSSE

Chilling time: 6 hours
Serves: 6

295g (10½ oz) Toblerone, broken into pieces, reserving one piece for decoration

6 tablespoons boiling water

275ml (10fl oz) crème fraîche

2 egg whites

Place the chocolate and the boiling water in a heatproof bowl suspended over a saucepan of barely simmering water and allow the chocolate to melt slowly. Remove from the heat, cool until it thickens and then fold in the crème fraîche. Whisk the egg whites until stiff peaks form and fold into the mixture. Chill in the fridge for at least 6 hours.

Once removed from the bean, the nibs are then roasted at over 100°C to develop the rich flavour and characteristic colour of cocoa.

The roasted nibs are then ground to produce cocoa mass (or cocoa liquor) which is made up of cocoa particles suspended in 50–55 per cent cocoa butter.

The cocoa mass is then transformed into chocolate by further processing and the addition of other ingredients. It can also be separated into cocoa powder and liquid cocoa butter.

'Cocoa solids' is the term used to describe the total amount of cocoa-derived material in a finished chocolate. The percentage of cocoa solids declared on chocolate packaging can refer to a combination of cocoa mass and extra cocoa butter, as in most chocolate bars, cocoa butter in white chocolate, or just cocoa mass, but this is rarely used on its own.

Cocoa Butter

Cocoa Mass

Cocoa Powder

Originally created by Eric Charot, whose restaurant, Interlude de Charot in Charlotte Street, London, gained a Michelin star within eleven months of opening, this unusual take on soup was discovered when the New Covent Garden Soup Co. marketing team was out 'researching' new recipes. Eating out was always one of the most enjoyable parts of their job and was considered to be a vital part of the creative process.

CHOCOLATE

SOUP

Preparation time: 30 minutes
Chilling time: 2 hours
Use: an electric whisk
Serves: 6

725ml (1¼ pints) milk

250ml (9fl oz) double cream

500g (18oz) dark chocolate, minimum 60% cocoa solids, coarsely chopped

50g (2oz) caster sugar

1 tablespoon water

8 large egg yolks

200ml (7fl oz) whipping cream

6 tablespoons skinned hazelnuts

rind of 1 orange, finely grated

6 teaspoons Grand Marnier

Bring the milk and double cream to the boil and add the chocolate. Set aside.

Heat the sugar with the water to make a syrup. When the sugar has melted, bring to the boil and boil for 1 minute. Start to whisk the egg yolks, then gradually pour the syrup over the yolks, whisking continuously.

Once the sugar has been incorporated, continue to whisk until the mixture is cold. The mixture will double in volume. Whip the cream and fold it in.

Mix the egg mixture with the chocolate sauce. Distribute the mixture between the individual bowls.

Preheat the oven to 200°C/400°F/gas mark 6.

Toast the hazelnuts on a tray in the oven. Watch them carefully after about 7 minutes as they burn easily.

Chill the soup for at least 2 hours.

Coarsely chop the hazelnuts and then sprinkle the hazelnuts and the grated orange zest over the soup and drizzle sparingly with Grand Marnier before serving as a starter.

HINT: Instead of adding the Grand Marnier and hazelnuts on top of the soup, try pouring a teaspoon of Grand Marnier in the bottom of the bowl, then some soup, followed by a layer of nuts and then the rest of the soup.

Inspired by the popularity of tarts, Isobel Wakemen transformed her reliable Chocolate and Seville Orange Mousse into this Moorish Tart, which brightens up the dark February days when Seville oranges, with their wizened and knarled skins and bitter flavour, are a truly seasonal treat.

MOORISH

TART

Preparation time: 30 minutes
Cooking time: 40 minutes
Chilling time: 3 hours
Use: 20cm (8in) tart tin

PASTRY

175g (6oz) plain flour

40g (1½ oz) icing sugar

125g (4½ oz) unsalted butter

grated zest of 1 Seville orange
(reserve the orange for the filling)

1 large egg, beaten

FILLING

150g (5oz) dark chocolate,
minimum 60% cocoa solids, broken into pieces

225ml (8fl oz) double cream

4 large egg yolks

50g golden caster sugar

juice of 1 Seville orange

Preheat the oven to 190°C/375°F/gas mark 5.

To make the pastry, process the flour, icing sugar, butter and orange zest in a food-processor to the breadcrumb stage or rub the ingredients together between your fingers. Add the beaten egg and mix until the pastry forms a ball. Wrap in greaseproof paper and leave to rest in the fridge for 30 minutes.

Roll out the pastry on a lightly floured board and place it in the tart tin. Prick the base with a fork and cover it with baking parchment and baking beans, bake it blind for 20 minutes, then remove the beans and the paper and continue to bake for a further 10 minutes. Remove from the oven and leave to cool.

Place the chocolate and the cream in a heatproof bowl suspended over a saucepan of barely simmering water.

To make the filling, beat the egg yolks and sugar together until light and fluffy. Stir the melted chocolate and cream together and then add the egg mixture. Replace the bowl over the saucepan of simmering water and stir until the mixture thickens. Add the orange juice and stir for about 2–3 minutes or until the mixture thickens again. Do not allow the mixture to boil. Pour into the cooled pastry case and chill until set.

HINT: Seville oranges freeze well, so if using straight from the freezer
grate the zest before thawing.

KUKUH

OR XOCOLATL

Theobroma, the genus that all cacao trees belong to, literally means 'food of the gods' from the Greek *theos* for 'god' and *broma*, meaning 'food or drink'. The Swedish naturalist Carolus Linnaeus named the tree in the eighteenth century in tribute to the Maya and Aztec drink.

In Mexico cocoa beans served as currency and the 'food of the gods' was also at the heart of many rituals and ceremonies. This heady, aromatic, cocoa beverage, *xocolatl* or *kukuh*, was favoured by Montezuma, the sixteenth-century king of the Aztecs, who drank it as a potent aphrodisiac. A simple infusion, it is spiced with chilli and thickened with ground corn.

On a recent trip to Belize, Cluny Brown, our marketing manager, was given a bowl of *kukuh* and was told how to make this refreshing, slightly watery drink. Cocoa beans are roasted on a *comal*, a smooth griddle, until their skins fall away, then they are ground together with a little corn and ground black pepper or dried, toasted chilli pepper. A little sugar is usually added, although in ancient times the Maya used forest honey. The drink can be served hot, tepid or cold, and given the extreme heat and humidity in Belize, it is delicious chilled and very different from the Western version we enjoy on cold winter days.

Auzibio Sho, who works at the Toledo Cocoa Growers Association in southern Belize, claims that not only is it good for general well-being, it is also great for inducing labour as well. *Kukuh* is also consumed for health and energy and is given to sick people and those who need to work hard.

To make this revitalising drink yourself, take a handful of cocoa beans and toast them on a griddle. Crack open the shells and remove the cocoa nibs. Grind the nibs in a pestle and mortar to a smooth paste and then stir in some freshly ground black pepper and ground corn. Take about a teaspoon of the paste and add enough water to make a large glass. Sweeten with sugar to taste. The Maya vary this drink by adding spices such as cinnamon, allspice and nutmeg.

HINT: Be warned. *Kukuh* is a very different drink to our traditional
sweet and creamy hot chocolate drink.

This cake is light and moist and the flavour of the chocolate and the almonds together with the texture and taste of the figs combine to make it truly unforgettable. Rachael Vingoe sent us this recipe, inspired by a cake that she bakes each Christmas.

CHOCOLATE, FIG AND ALMOND
CAKE

Preparation time: 20 minutes
Baking time: 50–60 minutes
Use: 23cm (9in) springform cake tin

150g (5oz) dried ready-to-eat figs

3 tablespoons Amaretto

250g (9oz) unsalted butter

250g (9oz) caster sugar

75g (3oz) ground almonds

100g (3½ oz) plain flour

4 large eggs

200g (7oz) dark chocolate, minimum 60% cocoa solids, chopped

3 heaped tablespoons cocoa powder

100g (3½ oz) whole peeled almonds

Preheat the oven to 180°C/350°F/gas mark 4. Butter and line the cake tin with greaseproof paper.

Remove the hard stalks from the figs and chop the figs in a food-processor into very small pieces. Place in a small bowl and pour the Amaretto over them. Set aside.

Cream the butter and the sugar until light and fluffy. Mix the ground almonds with the flour in a separate bowl. Beat the eggs and add a little at a time to the creamed mixture, beating gently between each addition. (If you are using an electric mixer it should be on its slowest speed.) Then add the almonds and flour a third at a time, continuing to beat gently.

Carefully fold in the chopped chocolate, the figs and Amaretto to the mixture.

Spoon the mixture into the cake tin and smooth over the top using a palette knife. Dust the top evenly with 2 heaped tablespoons of the cocoa. Arrange the whole almonds on top and then bake the cake for 50–60 minutes or until it is firm to the touch and a skewer inserted in the centre comes out clean. Leave to cool and then use a fine sieve to sprinkle the remaining cocoa over the top before serving.

HINT: Serve with freshly chopped coconut stirred into whipped cream.

If you are ever in Paris treat yourself to tea in the beautiful dining rooms at Ladurée on the Champs Élysées. Don't be put off by the queues and don't leave without an exquisitely wrapped box of the most famous macaroons in Paris.

CHOCOLATE

MACAROONS

Preparation time: 20 minutes
Cooking time: 10–12 minutes
Use: 2 large baking sheets, large pastry bag with 2cm (³/₄ in) nozzle

125g (4¹/₂ oz) ground almonds

25g (1oz) cocoa powder

250g (9oz) icing sugar

4 large egg whites, at room temperature

¹/₄ teaspoon vanilla extract

10g (¹/₂ oz) cocoa powder for dusting

GANACHE

see Micah's Truffles, page 147

Preheat the oven to 240°C/475°F/gas mark 9.

Butter the baking sheets and then line them with greaseproof paper or baking parchment with an overlap of about 2.5cm (1in) at either end. Prepare your pastry bag and nozzle.

Sift together the ground almonds, cocoa and 225g (8oz) of the icing sugar (reserving 25g/1oz of the icing sugar for the egg whites).

It is important that you have the correct amount of egg white for this recipe to work, so weigh out exactly 100g (3¹/₂ oz) by carefully adding part of the fourth egg white to the other three. The best way to do this is to whisk the fourth white in a cup with a fork and then add enough to the other whites to up the amount.

Whisk the egg whites until they are light and fluffy, add the reserved 25g (1oz) of icing sugar and continue to whisk until they are stiff and shiny but not dry. Gently fold the dry ingredients into the egg whites. Leave to rest for 10 minutes.

Stir the vanilla extract into the mixture, allowing it to deflate a little. This will help to stop the macaroons from cracking on top. Pour the mixture into the piping bag. Pipe the mixture on to the baking sheets in rounds the size of walnuts – try to make them as regular as possible. Tap the base of the baking sheets on a flat surface to remove some more of the air out of the macaroons. Sprinkle some cocoa on top of each one.

Put the first baking sheet on the top shelf of the oven and bake for 1 minute, and then reduce the temperature to 180°C/350°F/gas mark 4. Cook the macaroons for a further 10–12 minutes or until they are obviously cooked but not gooey and are still soft to the touch.

About 1 minute after you have removed the baking sheet from the oven gently lift one end of the paper and immediately pour a splash of hot water under the paper. The hot baking sheet causes the water to form steam and makes it easy to remove the macaroons. Carefully peel the macaroons from the paper and place on a wire rack to cool. Repeat the process with the second batch.

Once the macaroons have cooled, sandwich two together with the Ganache.

HINT: The secret is to use 'old' egg whites that have been kept uncovered in a fridge for at least a week.

Dodi Miller is passionate about chillies and is the driving force behind the company that has made the greatest variety and best-quality chillies available in the UK. She is also passionate about her Mole Poblano recipe and explains that it is a dish that can take a couple of days to prepare and that it is made for people you love, usually for festive occasions. There are many moles: green, red, yellow and black, but Poblano, the one with chocolate, is the most famous. The chocolate is used as a spice; it rounds off the edges of the chillies and gives the sauce a deep richness.

COOL CHILE Co.

MOLE POBLANO DE GUAJOLOTE

(dark chilli, nut and chocolate mole with turkey)

Preparation time: 2 hours
Cooking time: 1¹/₂ hours. Best left for a day before eating
Use: stockpot, large ovenproof pan
Serves: 8-10. For 12–16 use a 4.5–5.5kg (9–11lb) turkey and double the quantities for the mole

2.5–3kg (5–6¹/₂ lb) turkey (or a large chicken; the long slow cooking suits robust free-range birds)

STOCK

1 onion

1 carrot

1 stick celery

1 bay leaf

dried thyme

salt

pepper

MOLE

1 large beef tomato, roasted under the grill so the skin blackens, core removed

2 tablespoons sesame seeds, dry toasted

2 tablespoons coriander seeds, dry toasted

40g (1¹/₂ oz) dark chocolate,
minimum 60% cocoa solids, grated

125g (4¹/₂oz) mulato chillies

40g (1¹/₂ oz) ancho chillies

30g (1¹/₄ oz) pasilla chillies

75ml (3fl oz) duck/goose fat or lard, melted, or vegetable oil

40g (1¹/₂ oz) whole almonds, skin on

40g (1¹/₂ oz) raisins

1 small onion, peeled and chopped

2 garlic cloves, peeled and chopped

2 whole cloves (or pinch of ground clove)

5 peppercorns (or ¹/₄ teaspoon ground black pepper)

¹/₂ teaspoon ground cinnamon

2 stale corn tortillas or 2 stale pieces bread
(or use 2 tablespoons masa harina)

1 teaspoon salt

2 tablespoons sugar

¹/₄ teaspoon ground aniseed (or 1 star anise)

sesame seeds to garnish

Ask your butcher to portion the turkey, saving the carcass, trimmings and giblets to make the stock. You can also do this yourself: remove the wings, legs, thighs and breasts with the bones in, wrap and keep in the refrigerator. Put the carcass, wing tips and giblets into a stockpot, cover with water, add the onion, carrot, celery, bay leaf, a large pinch of dried thyme, salt and pepper. Simmer for 2 hours, partially covered, skim and strain to produce a rich, tasty stock.

To make the mole, chop the roasted tomato and put it into a bowl with the toasted sesame and coriander seeds and the grated chocolate.

To prepare the dried chillies, wipe off any dirt with a barely damp cloth. Pull out the stem and run your finger down the side to open the chilli out flat, shake out all the seeds and remove the membranes attaching them. Make a pile of flat pieces. Heat 2 tablespoons of the melted fat or oil in a frying pan over medium-high heat. Fry the chilli pieces one at a time for just a few seconds on either side; the colour will become tan. Do not overdo this, as the chillies will become very bitter. Drain as much of the fat back into the pan as you lift out the chillies and put them into a separate bowl. When you have finished frying all the chillies cover them with just boiled water using a weighted bowl to keep them submerged. Put to one side and soak for 1 hour, then drain.

Using the pan that you fried the chillies in, add a little more fat if necessary and fry the almonds until golden, drain and add to the bowl with the tomato. Next fry the raisins until they puff, drain and add to the bowl, then fry the onions and garlic until brown, drain and add to the bowl. Add the cloves, black pepper and cinnamon to the pan, fry for 1 minute and then add them to the bowl as well. Lastly tear the stale corn tortillas into pieces, fry, drain and add them to the tomato mix. Or mix the masa harina in with a little bit of the tomato mix and then stir it into the rest of the mix. Keep adding a little more fat as you need it.

Put a quarter of the tomato mixture into a blender with about 75ml (3fl oz) stock and blend until smooth. Pass through a sieve into a clean bowl and repeat with the rest of the tomato mixture. It should be a thick paste with only enough stock added to allow the mix to blend easily.

Next purée the drained chillies, a quarter at a time, adding 75ml (3fl oz) stock to allow the mix to blend easily. Pass through a sieve into a separate bowl. Do this until all the chillies have been puréed.

Pat the turkey pieces dry using paper towel. Heat 2 tablespoons of the melted fat or oil in a high-sided pan and brown the turkey on all sides, working in batches if necessary. Remove the pieces to an ovenproof casserole.

When complete, drain away most of the fat, leaving a little, and get the pan hot. Add the chilli purée, stirring all the time, letting it bubble and sear, darken and thicken. This takes about 5 minutes. Then add the tomato-based purée and simmer for about 2 minutes. Add 700ml (1¼ pints) of the stock, reduce the heat and simmer the sauce for 45 minutes. Then add 1 teaspoon salt and 2 tablespoons sugar or to taste. The sauce should coat the back of a spoon – add a little more stock if it is too thick.

Preheat the oven to 180°C/350°F/gas mark 4. Pour the sauce over the turkey pieces, add the aniseed or star anise, cover with a lid or foil and place in the oven for 1½ hours until the turkey is tender.

Serve sprinkled with toasted sesame seeds, accompanied with rice, corn tortillas and a watercress salad. Be generous with the sauce over the turkey.

HINT: The Cool Chile Co. can be contacted on tel: 0870 902 1145, fax: 0870 162 3923
email: orders@coolchile.co.uk

WICKED

The rainforest is the perfect environment for the cacao tree, which likes rich soil, humidity and shade.
It is rare to find *Theobroma cacao* growing outside a band 20 degrees north and 20 degrees south of the Equator.

Angela Reid remembers making this recipe with her grandmother in late September when she used to decant the damson gin to make way for the coming year's batch. The fruit left behind was so good you just could not throw it away. This is Angela's favourite of the many recipes devised to use up the drunken damsons. If you are not using damsons rescued from your own damson gin, we have adapted this recipe so that you can use fresh plums instead as we have done.

DRUNKEN DAMSON

DESSERT

Preparation time: 20 minutes if you have damson gin, 2 hours 20 minutes if making with plums
Cooking time: 12 minutes for a pie, 6 minutes for ramekins
Use: 20cm (8in) shallow pie dish or 8 ramekins
Serves: 8

DRUNKEN PLUMS
(if you are not using your own damsons in gin)

8 large plums, stoned and halved

2 tablespoons water

50g (2oz) caster sugar

4 tablespoons gin

FILLING

100g (3½oz) caster sugar

8 medium eggs

500g (18oz) dark chocolate,
minimum 60% cocoa solids, broken into pieces

250g (9oz) unsalted butter

200g (7oz) stoned damsons in gin
(if you are not using the plums above)

Preheat the oven to 200°C/400°F/gas mark 6. Butter the pie dish or ramekins.

To make the drunken plums, poach them gently in the sugar and water for about 10 minutes. Remove from the heat, stir in the gin and leave to cool and marinate for about 2 hours.

Whisk together the eggs and sugar until pale and creamy. Melt the chocolate and butter in a heatproof bowl suspended over a saucepan of barely simmering water. Mix the chocolate mixture and the drained fruit into the egg and sugar mixture. Pour into the dish or divide between the ramekins ensuring that there is fruit in each one.

Bake for 12 minutes for the pie dish or 6 minutes for the ramekins, until firm to the touch, but still slightly wobbly. Leave to cool and serve with your favourite cream.

HINT: If you are tempted to drizzle a little left-over gin over this pudding, beware.
It is far too strong and will overwhelm the chocolate and fruit flavours.

WICKED

White Chocolate

When we make our Dark Chocolate with 70% cocoa solids, we begin by mixing together cocoa mass, raw cane sugar and Bourbon vanilla to our own special recipe.

This mixture is then refined through a series of rollers that grind the particles of cocoa, sugar and vanilla so finely that they cannot be felt on the tongue. This process also continues to develop the flavour of the chocolate.

The next stage is the conching, which cannot be hurried and is a vital stage in the production of quality chocolate. A conching vessel, named after the conch shell-shape of the first prototype, controls the temperature and stirs the chocolate to create a smooth, velvety texture. The volatile acids are driven off and the flavour of the chocolate matures.

Extra cocoa butter is added at the end of conching to make the chocolate super smooth and to help it to melt more easily in the mouth.

The ultimate indulgence after a cold walk, this recipe can be made simpler by omitting the cinnamon or the cream but the drink will be less rich.

LUXURY

COCOA

Preparation time: 15 minutes
Makes: 1 standard mug

200ml (7fl oz) full-cream milk

2 tablespoons double cream

2 sticks cinnamon about 5cm (2in long)

3 teaspoons cocoa powder

2 teaspoons unrefined cane sugar

Put the milk, cream and cinnamon sticks into a pan and slowly bring to the boil. For a fuller cinnamon flavour leave the cinnamon sticks to infuse in the milk and cream mixture for 10 minutes once it has boiled and the heat has been turned off. Then reheat the mixture before pouring it into the mug. If you do this you do not need to put the cinnamon sticks into the finished drink.

Mix the cocoa with a splash more milk in a mug to form a paste.

Pour the just boiled milk mixture through a sieve into the mug, stirring to blend the paste with the milk.

Add the sugar and stir well.

Retrieve the cinnamon sticks from the sieve and submerge into the hot chocolate, if liked.

HINT: If you like cardamom, try substituting the cinnamon with the black seeds from inside one or two green cardamom pods, slightly crushed with the back of a spoon. Allow the seeds to infuse for 10 minutes before reheating, then sift the mixture into the mug.

White chocolate is one of those things that people either love or loathe, but good-quality chocolate made with real vanilla and cocoa butter will taste very different to the flavour most people are accustomed to. Not surprisingly, children love this sweet recipe from Jenny Phillips.

BANANA
AND WHITE CHOCOLATE CAKE

Preparation time: 20 minutes
Cooking time: 35 minutes
Use: 2 x 18cm (7in) cake tins

CAKE

175g (6oz) unsalted butter

175g (6oz) caster sugar

3 large eggs

2 ripe bananas, mashed

250g (9oz) self-raising flour

$^1/_2$ teaspoon baking powder

FILLING

2 bananas

juice of 1 lemon

1 tablespoon rosewater

150ml (5fl oz) crème fraîche

ICING

200g (7oz) good-quality white chocolate, broken into pieces

40g (1$^1/_2$ oz) unsalted butter

Preheat the oven to 180°C/350° F/gas mark 4. Brush the baking tins with melted butter and dust with flour.

Cream together the butter and sugar, whisk in the eggs and the mashed banana. Sift the flour and baking powder into the mixture and fold in well.

Divide the batter between the two tins and bake for about 40 minutes. Leave the cakes in the tins for 10 minutes, then turn out on a wire rack to cool.

To make the filling slice the bananas very thinly and toss in the lemon juice.

Mix the rosewater into the crème fraîche and spread this on to one of the cooled cake rounds, top with the sliced bananas and sandwich the two cakes together.

Melt the chocolate and the butter in a heatproof bowl suspended over a saucepan of barely simmering water.

Spread the melted chocolate mixture evenly over the top and sides of the cake, starting by pouring it into the centre of the top of the cake and spreading it with a palette knife until it begins to dribble down the sides of the cake.

Hint: Use fresh flowers placed in a test tube to decorate your cake.
Chocolate Cosmos has a wonderful chocolate scent and deep brown colour,
while shockingly pink sweet peas look beautiful with a chocolate glaze.

What would we do without those little books crammed with recipes from enthusiastic cooks compiled to raise money for schools and charities? This recipe, from the Bergvliet Road Nursery School in Cape Town, South Africa, has that Sixties ring to it – it is sweet and very rich and, together with a cup of tea, is guaranteed to hit the spot.

COFFEE, CHOCOLATE
AND WALNUT CAKE

Preparation time: 25 minutes
Cooking time: 25 minutes
Use: 2 x 18cm (7in) sandwich tins
Serves 10

225g (½lb) unsalted butter

225g (8oz) golden caster sugar

4 large eggs

200ml (7fl oz) strong fresh coffee, cooled

4 teaspoons cocoa powder

225g (8oz) self-raising flour

175g (6oz) walnuts, chopped

walnuts for decorating

FILLING AND ICING

Nigella's Blond Icing (see page 181)

Preheat the oven to 190°C/375°F/gas mark 5. Butter and flour the two tins.

Cream the butter and caster sugar until light and fluffy, add the eggs, one at a time, whisking well between each addition. Mix in the coffee. Sift the cocoa and self-raising flour together and add to the mixture, whisking everything well. Don't worry if the mixture has curdled slightly as it will come together once baked. Fold in the chopped walnuts and divide the mixture between the two tins. Bake in the oven for 25 minutes. Leave to cool in the tins for a few minutes before turning out and transferring to a wire rack to cool completely before filling and icing. Decorate with walnut pieces.

Hint: This cake should be handled carefully as it can break easily.

'Folks who like to fume and fuss are like a rocking chair; they use a lot of energy but don't get anywhere.' Kim Potter's great-aunt Lucille wrote *A Collection of 62 Years of Marriage*, a book of recipes and some wonderful words of wisdom. She was a sweet and strong-willed lady who, well into her nineties, thought nothing of jumping into her car and driving hundreds of miles. This is one of Kim's favourite recipes, adapted to include chocolate.

AUNT LUCILLE'S

PUMPKIN & MAYA GOLD BREAD

Preparation time: 30 minutes
Cooking time: 50 minutes–1 hour
Use: 22 x 12cm (9 x 5in) loaf tin
Makes: 1 loaf (14 slices)

350g (12oz) granulated sugar

50g (2oz) unsalted butter, softened

2 large eggs

225g (8oz) peeled and grated raw pumpkin or butternut squash

400g (14oz) plain flour

1/2 teaspoon bicarbonate of soda

1/2 teaspoon salt

1/2 teaspoon baking powder

1/2 teaspoon ground nutmeg

1/2 teaspoon allspice

1/2 teaspoon cinnamon

1/4 teaspoon ground cloves

60ml (2 1/2 fl oz) water

50g (2oz) Maya Gold, or other good-quality dark orange chocolate, chopped

Preheat the oven to 180°C/350°F/gas mark 4. Brush the loaf tin with melted butter and dust with flour.

Cream the butter and sugar until light and fluffy. Add the eggs, one at a time, beating well between each addition, then add the grated pumpkin and mix well.

Sift together the flour, bicarbonate of soda, salt, baking powder and all the spices and stir into the pumpkin mixture alternating with the water, until everything is incorporated.

Spoon about half the mixture into the loaf tin. Sprinkle about half the chocolate pieces on top of the mixture then cover them with the remainder of the mixture. Dig into the mixture with a spoon, parting it to form a trench along the top of the loaf and fill with the remainder of the chocolate, allowing some of the chocolate to remain on top of the loaf. Smooth over the hole with the spoon. The chocolate will melt as the loaf cooks and create a fault line through the loaf.

Bake in the oven for 50 minutes–1 hour. Cover with foil after 30 minutes to prevent the top from burning. Depending on how moist your pumpkin is you may need to bake this bread for a little longer. Test by inserting a skewer into the centre: if it comes out clean (although there might be melted chocolate left on the skewer), the loaves are cooked. Turn on to a wire rack and leave to cool before serving.

HINT: This loaf is delicious when sliced and lightly toasted with butter.
The easiest way to grate the pumpkin or squash is to use the grater attachment on your food-processor.

'You may lose the thread of your thoughts when you savour one of these sun-filled Mediterranean dates,' writes Marialuisa Rea Faggionato from Padua in Italy. She stuffs the dates with an orange- and lemon-flavoured marzipan, coats them in dark chocolate and serves them chilled for dessert. Marialuisa was a runner-up in one of our recipe competitions.

MEDITERRANEAN
THOUGHT-STEALING DATES

Preparation time: 30 minutes
Cooling time: 30 minutes
Use: wire rack
Makes: 30

30 dates

60g (2¹/₂ oz) peeled whole almonds

60g (2¹/₂ oz) caster sugar

finely grated zest of 1 orange,
plus a little of the juice

20ml (³/₄ fl oz) Limoncello
(Italian liqueur flavoured with lemon zest)

150g (5oz) dark chocolate,
minimum 60% cocoa solids, broken into pieces

Stone the dates. Chop the almonds finely and mix them with the sugar and orange zest. Add the Limoncello and knead to a malleable marzipan, adding a little orange juice if required. Stuff the dates with the marzipan mixture.

Melt the chocolate in a heatproof bowl suspended over a saucepan of barely simmering water. Dip the ends of the dates into the chocolate, leaving the centre bare, or dunk them to coat completely. Dip them twice if you like. Leave in a cool place to harden before serving.

HINT: Try to use fresh dates for this recipe, but if you can't find them,
choose dates that have been coated in as little syrup as possible.

This recipe started life as an almond tart with strawberries. They were replaced by pears, then chocolate was added and lastly the ginger appeared. Hazel Neil likes to adapt recipes depending on seasonal availability and the contents of her store cupboard. Next time she will try plums.

CHOCOLATE, PEAR AND GINGER
TART

Preparation time: 40 minutes
Chilling time: 30 minutes
Cooking time: 1 hour
Use: 28cm (11in) loose-based tart tin
Serves: 8

SHORTCRUST PASTRY

250g (9oz) plain flour

1 teaspoon salt

110g (4oz) unsalted butter

2 large egg yolks

4–5 tablespoons cold water

FILLING

125g (4½ oz) unsalted butter

125g (4½ oz) caster sugar

2 large eggs

100g (3½ oz) dark chocolate, minimum 60% cocoa solids, broken into pieces

1 dessertspoon finely chopped preserved ginger in syrup

25g (1oz) plain flour

125g (4½ oz) ground almonds

4 pears, just ripe, peeled

apricot jam for glaze

TO SERVE

Simple Chocolate Sauce, see page 61

Preheat the oven to 180°C/350°F/gas mark 4.

To make the pastry, sift the flour and salt into a large bowl. Cut the butter up into chunks and rub into the flour using your fingers until it resembles breadcrumbs. In a small bowl whisk together the egg yolks and the cold water briefly and then add to the mixture. Mix together until they come together as a ball. Wrap the dough in greaseproof paper and leave in the fridge to rest for about 30 minutes, before rolling out to line your tart tin. Bake the pastry blind by covering it with greaseproof paper and filling with baking beans for about 15–20 minutes or until lightly coloured.

Remove the pastry from the oven and lower the temperature to 160°C/325°F/gas mark 3.

To make the filling, cream the butter and sugar until light and fluffy. Beat the eggs, then add slowly and mix well. Melt the chocolate in a heatproof bowl suspended over a saucepan of barely simmering water. Allow to cool for a few minutes. Add the chocolate to the mixture along with the ginger. Mix in the flour and the almonds. Leave to cool before spreading over the pastry base.

Halve the pears, remove the cores and slice into wedges. Arrange in a fan shape on top of the chocolate mixture and press in slightly. Bake for about 30–40 minutes. Test that the filling is cooked by inserting a skewer into the centre which should come out clean.

Brush with apricot jam while still warm and serve warm or cold, with chocolate sauce or cream.

Andrea Longman invented these crumbly and buttery slices for a vegan friend as a thank-you present. They can be made with vegan margarine and are now a regular feature of her Christmas cookie cooking bonanza and are her friend's favourite Christmas present. If you make these for children, use milk chocolate instead.

SCRUMMY
CHOCOLATE SWIRL SHORTBREAD

Preparation time: 20 minutes
Cooking time: 25 minutes
Use: baking tray
Makes: 14

SHORTBREAD 1

150g (5oz) plain flour

$^1/_2$ teaspoon salt

50g (2oz) caster sugar

125g (4$^1/_2$oz) unsalted butter or vegan margarine

SHORTBREAD 2

125g (4$^1/_2$oz) plain flour

25g (1oz) cocoa powder

$^1/_2$ teaspoon salt

50g (2oz) caster sugar

125g (4$^1/_2$oz) unsalted butter or vegan margarine

100g (3$^1/_2$oz) dark chocolate, minimum 60% cocoa solids, or milk chocolate, preferably 34% cocoa solids, chopped into pieces

Preheat the oven to 150°C/300°F/gas mark 2.

To make the first shortbread, sift together the flour, salt and sugar. Rub in the butter until the mixture combines. Knead lightly, then place the dough in the fridge for 30 minutes before rolling out.

Follow the same step for the second shortbread, but include the cocoa with the flour.

Roll out both doughs on a lightly floured surface into equal-sized rectangles about 1cm ($^1/_2$in) thick. Place the plain shortbread on a sheet of greaseproof paper, place the chocolate shortbread on top of the plain one and then put the bigger pieces of chocolate onto the middle of the shortbread and scatter the smaller shards over the rest of the surface.

Carefully roll the shortbread like a Swiss roll, as tightly as possible, using the greaseproof paper to support it. (Don't worry if it breaks or the chocolate pokes through.) Once rolled, pinch both ends together to prevent the chocolate falling out, then using both hands, squeeze until it is 22cm long.

Using a very sharp knife slice the roll into 1cm ($^1/_2$in) slices. Lay well spaced on to a baking tray lined with baking parchment. Bake for 25 minutes, or until the plain shortbread has darkened slightly to a light golden colour. Cool on a wire rack.

HINT: These biscuits are clumsy and rustic-looking rather than elegant.

A British speciality dating back to the Middle Ages, fruit cakes have been baked for celebrations, weddings and at Christmas since the early eighteenth century. This twist on a traditional fruit cake is a bewitching creation by Stuart Oetzmann. His bakery, The Handmade Food Company, supplies the classiest food outlets in England with the most exquisite pies and pastries.

FRUIT
CAKE

Preparation time: 1 hour
Cooking time: 1 hour 15 minutes
Macerating time: 24 hours in advance
Use: 2 x 22 x 12cm (9 x 5in) loaf tins

175g (6oz) raisins

100g (3½ oz) currants

200g (7oz) stoned prunes

115g (4oz) candied orange, lemon or grapefruit peel (preferably home-made)

100ml (3½ fl oz) brandy

50ml (2fl oz) Morgan's Spiced Rum

275g (10oz) unsalted butter, softened

350g (12oz) muscovado sugar

3 medium eggs

200g (7oz) self-raising flour

150g (5oz) plain flour

1 teaspoon cinnamon

¼ teaspoon mace

¼ teaspoon ground cloves

¼ teaspoon ground ginger

100ml (3½ fl oz) espresso coffee

125g (4½ oz) walnuts

250g (9oz) dark chocolate, minimum 60% cocoa solids, chopped

Soak the fruit in half the brandy and all of the rum, 24 hours in advance of cooking.

Preheat the oven to 160°C/325°F/gas mark 3.

Butter the tins and line with greaseproof paper or baking parchment.

Cream the butter and the sugar. Add the eggs, one at a time, beating thoroughly with additions until each egg is well incorporated before adding the next. Sift the flours and spices together. Add to the mixture in two stages ensuring it is well combined between each addition. Fold in the fruit and the coffee. Finally add the walnuts and the chocolate and mix thoroughly, divide between the two tins, cover loosely with greaseproof paper or baking parchment and make a hole the size of a 50-pence piece in the top of the paper to allow the steam to escape. Cover with foil, making another hole, and tucking it under at the sides. Bake for 1 hour 15 minutes, checking the cake after about 1 hour. A skewer inserted into the centre should come out dry with a few crumbs clinging to the tip.

Leave the cakes to cool in their tins for 30 minutes and then turn out, peel off the paper and pour over the remaining brandy.

HINT: If you are making this several months in advance for a special occasion, wrap it with foil and douse regularly with brandy.

This pudding is a mint chocolate lover's dream dessert with its light soufflé texture and warm sauce oozing from the centre. Nicola Oaten started baking chocolate cakes at the age of five and has been experimenting ever since. This is her favourite recipe.

MINI HOT CHOCOLATE PUDDINGS

WITH A HINT OF MINT

Preparation time: 30 minutes
Cooking time: 10 minutes
Use: 4 small pudding bowls or dariole moulds, 6cm (2½ in) diameter and 5cm (2in) deep
Serves: 4

50g (2oz) dark chocolate, minimum 60% cocoa solids, broken into pieces

50g (2oz) mint chocolate

100g (3½ oz) unsalted butter

2 large eggs

2 large egg yolks

2 tablespoons golden caster sugar

6 tablespoons plain flour

Preheat the oven to 220°C/425°F/gas mark 7 if you intend to cook the puddings as soon as they are prepared. If you are cooking the puddings from frozen, preheat the oven to 180°C/350°F/gas mark 5. Lightly butter and flour the pudding bowls or dariole moulds.

Put the two chocolates and butter in a heatproof bowl suspended over a saucepan of barely simmering water.

Heat until the chocolate begins to melt then turn off the heat. Continue to stir until melted and then leave to cool.

Meanwhile put the eggs and egg yolks in a bowl with the sugar and whisk until frothy. When the chocolate mixture has cooled, fold it into the egg mixture. Sift in the flour and fold again. Pour into the prepared moulds filling them to the top, level off with a palette knife and bake for 10 minutes, if serving immediately. Alternatively they can be frozen or stored in the fridge for up to 1 day. Puddings cooked direct from the fridge will need an extra 2 minutes in the oven at 220°C/425°F/gas mark 8, frozen puddings need 12 minutes at the lower temperature directed above. The puddings will rise and be soft and gooey in the middle when ready.

Loosen from the moulds using a knife and turn out into the palm of your hand, place on individual plates. Dust with a mixture of cocoa powder and icing sugar.

HINT: Fill the moulds right to the top for a tall, elegant pudding.

At Green & Black's we prefer the French style of truffle which is predominantly a chocolate ganache, dusted with cocoa powder. They were first called truffles in the 1920s because they looked like real, freshly dug truffles, which are a fungus whose fruiting body grows underground. Belgian truffles often have a sweet, soft, light and creamy centre, which is very rich and filling.

MICAH'S

TRUFFLES

Preparation time: 30 minutes
Chilling time: minimum 3 hours or overnight
Makes: 36

275g (10oz) dark chocolate, minimum 60% cocoa solids, broken into pieces

250ml (9fl oz) double cream

50g (2oz) unsalted butter, at room temperature

50g (2oz) cocoa powder

Place the chocolate in a large bowl. Bring the cream to the boil and pour it over the chocolate. Stir gently until the chocolate has melted, trying not to create bubbles. Leave to cool for 2 minutes, then add the butter in two stages and stir in gently. Once the butter is incorporated, the ganache should be smooth and glossy with no oil slick on the surface. If the mixture splits and an oil slick appears, put the whole lot in a food processor and blend briefly until the mixture re-emulsifies. Set the truffle mixture in the fridge for a minimum of 3 hours or overnight.

Remove the ganache from the fridge about 15 minutes before you want to make the truffles, depending on room temperature. Put the cocoa into a bowl. Ensure your hands are cold and dry, then dust them with cocoa. Take spoonfuls of the ganache mixture (use a teaspoon or a tablespoon, depending on how large you like your truffles) and roll the mixture into a ball in your cocoa-dusted hands. Drop each shaped truffle into the bowl of cocoa, turn it around and then toss it between your palms to remove any excess powder. The truffles can then be returned to the fridge and kept for up to 2 days as long as they are stored in an airtight container.

HINT: These truffles can be eaten directly from the fridge or allowed to come to room temperature. The colder the truffle, the less dry and dusty the cocoa will seem when eating it.

ABRACADABRA

The complex flavour of chocolate is created by 550 flavour compounds found in cocoa after fermentation, drying, roasting and conching – far more than in most foods. A carrot has 96 flavour compounds.

TEMPERING

To mould chocolate or cover a cake in a hard chocolate shell that will set with a glossy shine, you have to temper the chocolate first, in exactly the same way we mould our chocolate bars.

Tempering involves melting, cooling and then reheating the chocolate, ensuring that all the tiny fat crystals in the chocolate are stable. If the fat crystals are not stable, the chocolate will set with white streaks or bloom. It will also be dull and won't have a good snap – the sound that good chocolate makes when you break it.

HOW TO TEMPER CHOCOLATE

To temper chocolate you need to use a minimum of 300g (10½ oz) of dark, milk or white chocolate. Any excess can always be stored and re-used another time.

Grate about 40g (1½ oz) of chocolate and set it aside. Break the remainder of the chocolate into pieces and melt in a bowl suspended over a saucepan of gently simmering water; do not allow the base of the bowl to come into direct contact with the water. Once the chocolate is completely melted, check the temperature using a digital thermometer. It should be between 55–58°C (131–136°F) for dark chocolate, 45–50°C (113–122°F) for milk and white chocolate.

Remove the chocolate from the heat and place over a bowl of cold water at about 21°C (70°F). Allow to cool, while occasionally stirring, until the temperature of the chocolate drops to 34°C (93°F).

Gently stir in the reserved grated chocolate and continue stirring until all the chocolate has melted and the temperature has cooled to 32–33°C (89–91°F).

The final temperature for dark chocolate should be about 30–32°C (86–90°F), between 28–30°C (82–86°F) for milk and 28–29°C (82–84°F) for white chocolate.

To test whether you have tempered your chocolate correctly, dip the tip of a palette knife in the chocolate and then leave it to cool and set for about 5 minutes. Properly tempered chocolate will be smooth with an even colour on the top, and if you peel the chocolate off the palette knife, the bottom will appear shiny. You can always start again using the same chocolate if you have failed to temper it properly.

Use the tempered chocolate immediately and quickly, leaving it over a pan of warm water while you work with it.

For a less technical method, see page 9.

This impressive, rich, chocolate cake is incredibly easy to make and guaranteed to launch your guests into orbit. It can also be made by replacing some of the dark chocolate with Maya Gold Chocolate to give the cake a hint of orange and spice. For an extra-special occasion, shake or brush edible gold dust (available from specialist cookshops) over it.

DARK CHOCOLATE MOUSSE CAKE

WITH GOLD DUST

Preparation time: 10 minutes
Cooking time: 35–45 minutes
Use: 20cm or 23cm (8in or 9in) cake tin with removable base or a similar-sized tart tin
Serves: 10

1 tablespoon ground almonds, plus extra for dusting the tin

300g (10$\frac{1}{2}$oz) dark chocolate, minimum 60% cocoa solids
or 200g (7oz) dark chocolate and 100g (3$\frac{1}{2}$oz) Maya Gold Chocolate, or other good-quality dark orange chocolate, broken into pieces

275g (10oz) caster sugar

165g (5$\frac{1}{2}$oz) unsalted butter

pinch of sea salt

5 large eggs

icing sugar or gold dust

Preheat the oven to 180°C/350°F/gas mark 4. Brush the tin with a little melted butter and dust with the ground almonds, shaking off any excess.

Melt the chocolate, caster sugar, butter and salt in a heatproof bowl suspended over a saucepan of barely simmering water, then remove from the heat.

Whisk the eggs with the ground almonds and fold into the chocolate mixture. The mixture will thicken after a few minutes. Pour into the cake tin and bake for 35–40 minutes.

Remove the sides of the tin and leave the cake on the base to cool, then dust using a fine sieve with icing sugar or brush with edible gold dust.

HINT: This cake will not rise much – it should be rich and thin.
If chilled overnight it will be dense, fudgey and wicked!

Micah Carr-Hill, our chocolate taster and product development chef, came back from one of his many forays in Italy with this dreamy idea. He visited the 'Salone del Gusto', a food fair that takes place in Turin every other autumn, and spent one evening at a dinner that had a chocolate theme. Make sure your Gorgonzola dolce is perfectly ripe, not too runny and not too hard and don't be afraid to pile on the chopped chocolate. The idea is that you taste the Gorgonzola first and then the chocolate begins to melt in your mouth and cuts through the richness, leaving you in a state of calm ecstasy.

GORGONZOLA DOLCE
WITH DARK CHOCOLATE

Preparation time: 5 minutes
Makes: 60 pieces

100g (3½ oz) dark chocolate,
minimum 60% cocoa solids

350g (12oz) Gorgonzola dolce

Chop the chocolate into medium-sized chunks, about the size of your thumbnail, using a sharp knife.

Cover the entire surface of the cheese with the chunks of chocolate, pressing it in gently.

Make sure that the cheese is densely covered, as you do need a high proportion of chocolate to cheese to get the full benefit of this recipe.

HINT: Don't store your cheese in the fridge because if the temperature is too low, the cold can impair the flavour. Wrap it in waxed paper or greaseproof or parchment paper and store it in a cool place.

Sally Johnston's brother-in-law had never tried to cook before he spent some time in a Canadian prison. A fellow prisoner gave him this simple recipe to cook for his wife when she visited him and it has since become a family favourite. He sent it to Sally in England and she passed it on to us.

INMATES'
CHOCOLATE CAKE

Preparation time: 20 minutes
Cooking time: 40 minutes
Use: 2 x 20cm (8in) cake tins with deep sides
Serves: 15–20

CAKE

500g (18oz) plain flour

500g (18oz) sugar

1 teaspoon bicarbonate of soda

1 tablespoon baking powder

$^1/_2$ teaspoon salt

150g (5oz) cocoa powder

150 ml ($^1/_4$ pint) buttermilk

150ml ($^1/_4$ pint) vegetable oil

4 large eggs

1 teaspoon vanilla extract

200ml (7fl oz) water

FILLING

340g (11$^1/_2$ oz) apricot jam

chocolate glaze (see page 180) or
chocolate fudge sauce (see page 61)

Preheat the oven to 180°C/350°F/gas mark 4. Butter and flour the baking tins.

Sift all the dry ingredients into a large mixing bowl. Add the remaining ingredients and whisk using a mixer or with a strong arm for about 3 minutes. Bake for 35–40 minutes. Leave to cool on a wire rack. Once cooled, sandwich together with apricot jam and pour over the chocolate glaze.

HINT: If you are in a hurry, use two large jars of chocolate spread to ice this cake.

A great classic, this recipe was picked up in the Eighties in Paris and originated in the famous Taillevent restaurant. It is delicious served with Mint Crème Anglaise (see page 61) and tuiles.

TAILLEVENT
TERRINE

Preparation time: 20 minutes
Freezing time: overnight
Use: 900g (2lb) loaf tin

225g (8oz) dark chocolate, minimum 60% cocoa solids, broken into pieces

100g (3½ oz) icing sugar

175g (6oz) softened unsalted butter

5 large eggs, separated

75g (3oz) cocoa powder

salt

185ml (6½ fl oz) whipping cream

Melt the chocolate in a heatproof bowl suspended over a saucepan of barely simmering water.

Stir in the icing sugar, then the butter. Whisk in the egg yolks and the cocoa. Add a pinch of salt. Whisk the egg whites until soft peaks form. Whip the cream until thick, then fold in the egg whites and the cream into the mixture, ensuring they are well incorporated.

Sprinkle water inside the loaf tin, line with clingfilm, pour the mixture into the tin and freeze overnight. Remove from the freezer for about 15 minutes before slicing into slabs and serving with the Mint Crème Anglaise on page 61.

HINT: This terrine can be kept in the freezer for up to a week.

Whole Earth Foods was started by Craig Sams, one of the pioneers of the organic movement, who was extolling the beliefs of macrobiotics and organic farming over thirty-five years ago when the majority of us had not even begun to think about the effects of conventional farming methods on the environment and our health. Cocoa Crunch, a naughty yet healthy breakfast cereal adored by adults and children alike, is one of the many delicious organic foods produced by Whole Earth.

COCOA

CRUNCH

Preparation time: 10 minutes
Cooking time: 35–40 minutes
Use: large roasting tin or baking tray
Makes: 750g (1lb 2oz)

250g (9oz) sugar

100ml (3¹/₂ fl oz) water

50ml (2fl oz) vegetable oil

75g (3oz) milk chocolate,
preferably 34% cocoa solids, chopped

2 teaspoons honey

375g (13oz) oats

110g (4oz) Rice Crispies (or puffed rice cereal)

25g (1oz) desiccated coconut

30g (1oz) cocoa powder

Preheat the oven to 180°C/350°F/gas mark 4.

Line a large baking tray with greaseproof paper or baking parchment.

Melt the sugar in the water over a low heat to make a syrup without caramelising it. Remember not to stir or disturb the sugar and water mixture at all while it is melting. Allow the syrup to cool until warm and then melt the vegetable oil and chocolate in the syrup. Add the honey to the syrup and mix well.

In a large bowl mix together the oats, Rice Crispies, coconut and cocoa together. Add the syrup mixture to the dry ingredients and mix thoroughly. Spread the mixture on to the prepared baking tray to a thickness of about 1cm (¹/₂in).

Bake for about 35–40 minutes, and using a fork, turn the Cocoa Crunch regularly. Be careful not to crush it into fine crumbs though; it should remain as chunks, like a granola.

It is better to undercook the Cocoa Crunch as it will burn easily, especially around the sides of the baking tray, so do watch it.

HINT: Dip the spoon you are going to use to measure the honey in some oil
to prevent the honey from sticking to the spoon.

This crumbly biscuit from Brittany is traditionally a plain biscuit which has so much butter in it any other flavour seems superfluous. When working on some biscuit ideas we couldn't resist trying to rival the traditional English chocolate digestive with this ultra indulgent biscuit with a coating of our milk and dark chocolate.

BRETON
BUTTER BISCUITS

Preparation time: 10 minutes
Chilling time: 15 minutes
Cooking time: 15–20 minutes
Use: 5 cm (2½ in) fluted biscuit cutter
Makes: 50

375g (13oz) plain flour

large pinch of salt

150g (5oz) caster sugar

200g (7oz) unsalted butter, chilled and diced

1 large egg, lightly beaten

½ teaspoon vanilla extract

200g (7oz) milk chocolate or 50g (2oz) each of milk, dark, Maya Gold (or good-quality dark orange chocolate) and white chocolate, broken into pieces for dipping

Preheat the oven to 160°C/325°F/gas mark 3. Butter a large baking sheet.

Sift together the flour and the salt. Add the sugar and butter and process in a food-processor or rub between your fingertips until the mixture resembles breadcrumbs. Add the egg and the vanilla extract and process again or mix together with your hands until the mixture comes together as a firm dough. Wrap in clingfilm and chill for at least 15 minutes.

Roll out on a lightly floured board to a thickness of about 3 mm (⅛in). Cut out the biscuits using the fluted cutter.

Place on the baking sheet and bake for 15–20 minutes or until light golden brown. Cool on a wire rack.

Once the biscuits have cooled, melt the chocolate in a heatproof bowl suspended over a saucepan of barely simmering water. If using one flavour of chocolate, select a bowl that will allow you to fit your hand into it so that you can dip the biscuits. Be very careful when melting the white chocolate and ensure that the bowl does not touch the water as it will seize easily. If you are using different flavours of chocolate, once melted, pour the chocolate on to a small plate and dip the surface of each biscuit in the chocolate before returning them to the wire rack to set.

The biscuits can simply have one surface dipped in the chocolate or you could decorate by drizzling white chocolate over a biscuit previously dipped in dark or white chocolate. You can also dip only half the biscuit with chocolate.

HINT: The most effective way of melting chocolate is to microwave it very slowly on medium in short bursts. To melt 50g (2oz), microwave for 30 seconds, then continue in 10-second bursts, stirring in between each one.

Jo Gilks finds there are times when she can't wait to tuck into a meaty stew with someone, as so many of her friends seem to have become vegans or vegetarians or developed allergies. This cake is part of the repertoire that enables her to feed them. Made with polenta, which is cornmeal rather than flour, it satisfies all those people whose wheat-free diets prevent them from eating many of the chocolate recipes she would usually make.

POLENTA CHOCOLATE
CAKE

Preparation time: 25 minutes
Cooking time: 40 minutes
Use: 35cm (10in) springform, deep-sided cake tin
Serves: 10

225g (8oz) dark chocolate, minimum 60% cocoa solids, broken into pieces

125g (4$\frac{1}{2}$ oz) unsalted butter

5 large eggs, separated

150g (5oz) caster sugar

100g (3$\frac{1}{2}$ oz) fine polenta

50ml (2fl oz) dark rum

Icing sugar for dusting

Preheat the oven to 180°C/350°F/gas mark 4. Butter and flour the cake tin.

Melt the chocolate and the butter in a heatproof bowl suspended over a saucepan of barely simmering water. Whisk together the egg yolks with 75g (3oz) of sugar until the mixture is thick and creamy. Fold into the chocolate mixture.

Whisk the egg whites with the remaining sugar until stiff peaks form. Stir the polenta and rum into the chocolate mixture and then fold in the egg whites. Spoon into the prepared cake tin and bake in the oven for about 40 minutes. Remove from the oven and leave the cake to cool in the tin (it will sink as it cools). Dust with icing sugar before serving.

HINT: For a crisp crust, add all the sugar to the egg yolks and whisk the egg whites without any sugar.

This tart, with its crumbly, buttery base, is a cross between a biscuit and a tart and is very easy to make. It can be filled with almost anything, although we think our creamy chocolate spread is the perfect match for the pine nuts.

ITALIAN PINE NUT TART
WITH CHOCOLATE SPREAD

Preparation time: 35 minutes
Chilling time: 45 minutes
Cooking time: 30–35 minutes
Use: 23cm (9in) fluted, loose-based tart tin
Serves: 6 8

PASTRY

310g (11oz) plain flour

1 teaspoon baking powder

100g (3½oz) unsalted butter, cold,
plus a little melted for greasing

150g (5oz) caster sugar

2 large eggs, beaten

2 tablespoons water

FILLING

300g (11oz) chocolate hazelnut spread

TOPPING

1 large egg yolk

1 tablespoon milk

3 tablespoons pine nuts

1 tablespoon icing sugar for dusting

Preheat the oven to 180°C/350°F/gas mark 4. Lightly brush over the tart tin with a little melted butter.

To make the pastry, sift the flour and the baking powder into a bowl and rub in the butter until the mixture resembles breadcrumbs. Add the sugar and then mix in the eggs and some of the water. Mix together using your hands and then form a ball. Turn on to a lightly floured board and knead gently using the heel of your hand until the mixture is smooth and even. Cover and chill for 45 minutes.

Roll out three-quarters of the pastry on a lightly floured board to a size larger than the tart tin. Press lightly into the prepared tart tin and trim. Spoon the chocolate spread into the pastry base to cover it. Roll out the remainder of the pastry and place it on top of the chocolate spread. Press the edges of the top and bottom pastry together to seal it.

To make the topping, beat together the egg yolk and the milk, then brush it over the top layer of pastry. Sprinkle the pine nuts evenly over the top of the tart and bake for 30–35 minutes until light brown. Dust with icing sugar and leave to cool before serving.

HINT: Pine nuts burn very quickly so keep an eye on this tart during the later stages of baking.

ABRACADABRA

These heavenly brownies are quick, easy and totally indulgent. They are perfect at tea-time or equally delicious served with crème fraîche as a treat after lunch or dinner with friends. Make sure you use the correct size baking or roasting tin and take care not to overcook them. As a rule, when you start to smell them they are usually close to being done: you are better off removing them too soon and putting them back, which does them no harm at all!

CHOCOLATE AND CHERRY
BROWNIES

Preparation time: 15 minutes
Cooking time: 25 minutes
Makes: 28 brownies
Use: 1 baking or roasting tin 34 x 25cm (13 x 10in) and at least 6cm (2^1/$_4$ in deep)

300g (11oz) unsalted butter

300g (10^1/$_2$ oz) dark chocolate, minimum 60% cocoa solids, broken into pieces

5 large eggs

450g (1lb) granulated sugar

1 tablespoon vanilla extract

200g (7oz) plain flour

1 teaspoon salt

250g (9oz) dried cherries

Preheat the oven to 180°C/350°F/gas mark 4. Line the baking tin with greaseproof paper or baking parchment.

Melt the butter and chocolate together in a heatproof bowl suspended over a saucepan of barely simmering water. Beat the eggs, sugar and vanilla extract together in a bowl until the mixture is thick and creamy and coats the back of a spoon. Once the butter and the chocolate have melted, remove from the heat and beat in the egg mixture. Sift the flour and salt together, then add them to the mixture, and continue to beat until smooth. Stir in the dried cherries.

Pour into the roasting tin, ensuring the mixture is evenly distributed in the tin. Bake in the oven for 20–25 minutes or until the whole of the top has formed a light brown crust that has started to crack. This giant brownie should not wobble, but should remain gooey on the inside.

Leave to cool for about 20 minutes before cutting into large squares while still in the pan. The greaseproof paper or baking parchment should peel off easily.

HINT: Try adding nuts or other dried fruits as an alternative to the cherries, or make plain chocolate brownies without any extras at all.

This cake is incredibly quick and easy to make and the ground cinnamon stick topping reminds us of why we should always freshly grind our spices. Melody Talbot has lived in New York, London, Sydney and Verbier and has always moved to her family's next destination with a batch of her favourite recipes. This one was scribbled on a scrap of paper at a gathering of mothers from her children's school in New York.

CHOCOLATE CHIP CAKE

WITH CINNAMON STICK TOPPING

Preparation time: 15 minutes
Cooking time: 50–60 minutes
Use: 1 x 23cm (9in) springform cake tin
Serves: 8

TOPPING

2 cinnamon sticks or 1 teaspoon ground cinnamon

75g (3oz) unsalted butter

4 tablespoons granulated sugar

CAKE

110g (4oz) unsalted butter, softened

220g (8oz) granulated sugar

2 large eggs

300ml (½ pint) sour cream or full-fat yogurt

1 teaspoon vanilla extract

450g (1lb) self-raising flour

200g (7oz) dark chocolate, minimum 60% cocoa solids, chopped

Preheat the oven to 180°C/350°F/gas mark 4. Butter and flour the cake tin.

To make the topping, grind the cinnamon sticks in a pestle and mortar until you have quite a fine powder with a few threads of the cinnamon stick remaining, as these give an added intensity of flavour.

Melt the butter and add the sugar and the cinnamon, stirring well. Set aside.

To make the cake, cream the butter and sugar, add the eggs and continue to beat until smooth. Add the sour cream or yogurt and the vanilla extract and mix well. Sift in the flour and add the chocolate. Stir.

Pour the batter into the cake tin, then evenly spread the topping over the batter using the back of a spoon.

Bake in the oven for 50–60 minutes. Leave to cool in the tin before turning out.

HINT: Try to find cinnamon from Sri Lanka or the Seychelles. Avoid cassia, which is often passed off as cinnamon, but has a much cruder flavour and a tougher bark.

OLD TIMERS

The rainforest has existed for at least 40 million years and although it now covers just 2 per cent of the earth's surface, 40 per cent of all species of animals and plants live there. By 1990, half of the world's rainforests had been destroyed and they are still being felled at an alarming rate of about 142,000 square kilometres per year.

This wonderfully simple Kuglòf recipe was given to Csilla Fodor by her Hungarian grandmother, Eszter, who still lives in Oroshàza in south-eastern Hungary. Csilla has fond memories of spending summer holidays with her as a child when this cake, speckled with chocolate, was a great luxury after the bland food of her strict boarding school.

HUNGARIAN

KUGLÒF

Preparation time: 30 minutes
Cooking time: 55 minutes
Use: 1 x 22cm (8in) kugelhof mould
Serves: 8

6 large eggs, separated

375g (13oz) sugar

200g (7oz) unsalted butter, softened

450g (1lb) flour

250ml (9fl oz) milk

1 teaspoon lemon juice

100g (3½ oz) dark chocolate, minimum 60% cocoa solids, grated

icing sugar for dusting

Preheat the oven to 140°C/275°F/gas mark 1.

Brush the inside of the mould thoroughly with a little melted butter. Dust with flour.

Whisk together the eggs yolks, sugar and the butter. Sift the flour and add it to the mixture together with the milk and the lemon juice, mix well. Whisk the egg whites until soft peaks form, then fold gently into the mixture. Divide the mixture in half and add the grated chocolate to one half of the mixture.

Spoon the plain mixture into the bottom of the mould, then top with the chocolate mixture. Bake for about 55 minutes or until the kuglof cracks slightly on the top.

Remove from the oven and leave to cool for about 10 minutes before turning out on to a wire rack. Once the kuglof is completely cooled, dust with icing sugar before serving.

HINT: To ensure the cake does not stick to the tin, place the mould in the freezer for 30 minutes before brushing with butter and then dusting with flour.

Claire Fry is the graphic designer who has worked on both the Green & Black's and New Covent Garden Soup Company brands. She loves baking cakes and often makes themed ones for close friends. Her 'Bandstand on Clapham Common' and 'The Royal Albert Hall' were both wedding cakes for couples who enjoyed walking their dogs and singing in a choir. This recipe is the one she claims is infallible and lends itself to different shapes. It is delicious filled with apricot jam and covered with butterscotch bar or fudge sauce.

DEVIL'S
FOOD CAKE

Preparation time: 15 minutes
Cooking time: 30–35 minutes
Use: 2 x 20cm (8in) sandwich tins with deep sides
Makes: 10–12 large slices

350g (12 oz) plain flour

1/2 teaspoon baking powder

2 teaspoons bicarbonate of soda

large pinch of salt

110g (4oz) cocoa powder

425g (15fl oz) cold water

225g (8oz) margarine or shortening

600g (20oz) caster sugar

4 large eggs

180g (7oz) apricot jam

Butterscotch or Fudge Sauce, see page 61

Preheat the oven to 180°C/350°F/gas mark 4.

Sift the flour with the baking powder, bicarbonate of soda and salt. Blend the cocoa with the water and set aside. Soften the margarine or shortening with a wooden spoon and add the sugar. Cream until light and very soft.

Whisk the eggs until frothy, add to the creamed mixture a little at a time and beat well. Stir in the flour alternately with the cocoa and water. Divide the mixture between the two tins and bake for 30–35 minutes or until a skewer inserted into the centre comes out clean. Leave to cool for a few minutes in the tin, then turn out on to a wire rack. Leave to cool completely before filling with apricot jam or a filling of your choice. Pour Butterscotch Sauce over the top and down the sides of the cake.

HINT: Don't be tempted to use butter when making this cake as it is definitely lighter and has a better texture made with margarine.

Treat your friends to three different *pôts de crème*. They are exceedingly rich so why not serve them in egg cups on a dessert plate with a coffee spoon and delicate Chocolate Tuiles (see page 106) or plain butter biscuits?

THREE PÔTS
DE CRÈME

Preparation time: 30 minutes
Chilling time: 2–3 hours
Use: egg cups or other small unusual containers – try liqueur glasses
Serves: 6

400ml (14fl oz) single cream

1 vanilla pod

25g (1oz) dark chocolate,
minimum 60% cocoa solids, broken into pieces

25g (1oz) Maya Gold Chocolate, or
other good-quality dark orange chocolate,
broken into pieces

50g (2oz) white chocolate, broken into pieces

6 large egg yolks

50g (2oz) sugar

¹/₂ level teaspoon salt

Gently heat the cream with the vanilla pod until bubbles begin to form at the edge, but ensuring the cream does not boil. Remove from the heat and set aside to infuse.

Melt the chocolates separately in heatproof bowls suspended over saucepans of barely simmering water. (Keep the saucepans of water as you will need them later on.) Leave the chocolates to cool, then beat two of the egg yolks into each of the melted chocolates until the mixtures are smooth. Stir one third of the sugar and salt into each chocolate mixture until completely dissolved.

Remove the vanilla pod from the cream and gently stir one third of the cream into each chocolate mixture until well blended. Replace the bowls over saucepans of simmering water.

Cook until each mixture coats the back of a spoon, stirring all the time.

Pour each chocolate mixture into your chosen containers and chill for about 2–3 hours or until the mixture has set.

HINT: Melt the chocolate before adding it to the cream. If you try to add chopped or grated chocolate to the hot mixture, it will seize and your pôts will be grainy.

'Celebrations' opened up a whole new market for chocolate makers and is one of those products that all marketeers wish they had thought of first. Jane Holden rather cheekily sent us this recipe for her 'Celebration Brownies' which she says 'will keep your visitors guessing as each brownie contains a different chocolate and therefore has a very different texture and flavour from the next one.' You will always find they will want more than one, so you may want to double the recipe.

CELEBRATION
BROWNIES

Preparation time: 20 minutes
Cooking time: 25–30 minutes
Use: 28 x 18cm (11 x 7in) baking tin
Makes: 15

200g (7oz) unsalted butter

100g (3½ oz) dark chocolate,
minimum 60% cocoa solids, broken into pieces

350g (12oz) dark soft brown sugar

4 large eggs

1 teaspoon vanilla extract

200g (8oz) self-raising flour

pinch of salt

280g (10¼ oz) box of 'Celebrations'
or other chocolates of your choice (see hint below)

Preheat the oven to 180°C/350°F/gas mark 4.

Brush the tin with melted butter, then line it with greaseproof paper.

Melt the butter and the chocolate in a heatproof bowl suspended over a saucepan of barely simmering water. Remove from the heat and add the sugar.

Beat the eggs and the vanilla essence and add to the chocolate mixture. Sift the flour and stir into the mixture with the salt.

Unwrap the chocolates. Pour half the mixture into the tin and then carefully place the chocolates so that there will be at least one in each portion once cut. Pour in the remaining mixture, ensuring that the chocolates are covered.

Bake for about 25–30 minutes until the top is crispy and the inside soft.

Leave to cool in the tin before cutting.

HINT: This recipe also works well with Maltesers dotted all around the tray
and then covered with the cake mixture, or try a layer of mint chocolate thins.

This recipe will find a home for those sad, brown bananas that nobody wants to eat. An old favourite, it is the perfect teatime treat and goes well with tea or coffee. It is also delicious using pecans instead of walnuts.

WHITE CHOCOLATE,
WALNUT AND BANANA LOAF

Preparation time: 30 minutes
Baking time: 1–1¼ hours
Use: 900g (2lb) loaf tin or 2 x 450g (1lb) tins
Makes: 1 large loaf or 2 medium loaves

125g (4½ oz) unsalted butter, melted

175g (6oz) plain flour

2 teaspoons baking powder

½ teaspoon bicarbonate of soda

½ teaspoon salt

150g (5oz) caster sugar

2 large eggs

4 small, ripe bananas, mashed

100g (3½ oz) good-quality white chocolate, chopped into large chunks

60g (2½ oz) walnuts, chopped

1 teaspoon vanilla extract

Preheat oven to 180°C/350°F/gas mark 4. Brush the inside of the loaf tin with a little melted butter, then dust with flour.

Mix the flour, baking powder, bicarbonate of soda and salt in a bowl. In a separate bowl whisk the melted butter and sugar together. Beat in the eggs, one at a time, then whisk in the mashed bananas. Add the white chocolate, walnuts and vanilla. Add the dry ingredients to the wet ingredients in three stages, stirring after each addition.

Pour into the loaf tin(s) and bake for 1–1¼ hours.

Slide a spatula around the edge of the loaf and leave in the tin to cool.

HINT: Nigella's Blond Icing (see page 181) is delicious poured over this cake.

You only have to spend a short time in the rainforest to understand why growing cacao organically makes sense. The cacao trees are planted under indigenous trees for shade, are sheltered from the wind and sun and don't dry out when it gets too hot. Any insect pests that eat the crop are picked off by natural predators.

The forest floor is a carpet of leaf litter which fills the soil with the nutrients that help the plants to grow without need of chemical fertilisers. This results in a bio-diverse environment where cacao trees thrive amongst forest flora and fauna.

Slashing and burning rainforest trees to intensify the cultivation of crops has destroyed large tracts of the rainforest. The natural pest predators cannot live without trees and so many of the conventional growers use chemical insect-killers and if these are not used carefully they can poison other wildlife or wipe out their food chains. Less leaf litter means the soil runs out of nutrients, so artificial fertilisers have to be used. If too much is used, the excess can run off into streams and rivers and pollute them, which harms the animals that live in and depend on the river water.

Konditor & Cook is the place we go to each day for our lunch. We try to resist as it is a bit of a luxury, but those beautiful, minimalist, pale blue bags keep appearing at lunch-time. Now and again eyeing up the pastries proves to be too much and one of us, unable to resist the temptation, buys one. This recipe for Chocolate Biscuit Cake was kindly given to us by chef Gerhard Jenne. We promised him we would never try to make it on a bigger scale!

KONDITOR & COOK
CHOCOLATE BISCUIT CAKE

Preparation time: 15 minutes
Chilling time: 4 hours
Use: 20 x 8cm (8 x 3in) loaf tin
Makes: 10 large, very rich slices

125g (4¹/₂oz) unsalted butter

75g (3oz) golden syrup

200g (7oz) dark chocolate,
minimum 60% cocoa solids, broken into pieces

1 egg

50g (2oz) digestive biscuits

50g (2oz) whole walnuts

50g (2oz) sultanas

50g (2oz) glacé cherries, reserving a few
for decoration

Line the loaf tin with greaseproof paper or baking parchment and set aside.

Melt the butter and syrup together in a small saucepan over a gentle heat until they begin to boil.

Melt the chocolate in a heatproof bowl suspended over a saucepan of barely simmering water, then mix thoroughly with the butter and golden syrup.

Pasteurise the egg by beating it slowly and continuously into the hot chocolate mixture.

Break up the biscuits into large chunks; remember, they will be broken further when mixed, so don't make them too small.

Add the walnuts, sultanas and most of the cherries.

Pour the chocolate mixture on to the dry ingredients and mix together with a spatula or wooden spoon.

Press the mixture into the tin and decorate with reserved glacé cherries. Leave to set in the fridge for about 4 hours. Remove from the fridge, peel off the paper and cut into slices or cubes. Serve chilled.

HINT: To make this recipe more appealing to children,
why not replace 100g of dark chocolate with milk chocolate?

DARK
ICING

Ideal for covering a sophisticated chocolate cake

100g (3^1/$_2$ oz) dark chocolate, minimum 60% cocoa solids, chopped

50g (2oz) unsalted butter, cubed

Melt the chocolate in a heatproof bowl suspended over a saucepan of barely simmering water. Remove from the heat, add the butter and stir until the butter has melted and the sauce has the consistency of thick pouring cream.

Use the back of a teaspoon to spread over the top and sides of the cake. Allow to set. If refrigerated the icing will lose its sheen.

CHOCOLATE
GLAZE

A traditional, sweet chocolate glaze

100g (3^1/$_2$ oz) dark chocolate, minimum 60% cocoa solids, chopped

40g (1^1/$_2$ oz) unsalted butter, cubed

3 tablespoons water

75g (3oz) icing sugar

Melt the chocolate in a heatproof bowl, suspended over a saucepan of barely simmering water. Leaving the bowl over the hot water, sift the icing sugar and add it to the melted chocolate, stir well, then add the butter and stir until fully incorporated. Remove the bowl from the heat and add the water, 1 tablespoon at a time. Use the glaze while it is still warm – it will run if it is too hot and it will not spread if it is too cold.

DUSKY BUTTER
ICING

Ideal for filling and covering a children's cake.

100g (3^1/$_2$ oz) milk chocolate

175g (6oz) unsalted butter

175g (6oz) icing sugar

Melt the chocolate in a heatproof bowl suspended over a saucepan of barely simmering water. Set aside to cool until tepid. Beat the butter until softened, add the sugar and beat together well. Add the chocolate to the mixture and beat together well.

ORANGE
DUST

A more unusual topping

4 oranges

300g (11oz) granulated sugar

120ml (4fl oz) water

oil for greasing

Scrub the oranges and pat them dry. Using a vegetable peeler, remove the top layer of peel, but ensure you don't remove the pith. Bring the sugar and the water to the boil and, without stirring, boil for about 10 minutes or until it begins to form a syrup (test by dropping some on to a plate; if it begins to set immediately it is ready). Add the orange peel and continue to boil without stirring for another 10 minutes. Brush some oil on to a baking sheet and, using a pair of tongs, transfer the caramelised peel to the baking sheet. Leave to cool and dry completely before pulverising in a food-processor. Store in an airtight container.

CHOCOLATE
GANACHE

A thick, rich and creamy filling or topping. If you need more,
simply increase the quantities, keeping the ingredients in the same proportions.

300g (10oz) dark chocolate,
minimum 60% cocoa solids, chopped

300ml (10fl oz) double cream

Put the chocolate into a large bowl. Heat the cream until it begins to simmer, pour it over the chocolate and immediately begin to whisk. Continue to whisk until the mixture has cooled and thickened.

NIGELLA'S BLOND
ICING

200g (7oz) white chocolate

50g (2oz) unsalted butter

220ml (8fl oz) crème fraîche

100g (3½oz) unrefined golden icing sugar, sifted

Melt the chocolate and the butter in a heatproof bowl suspended over a saucepan of barely simmering water. Remove and leave to cool a little, add the crème fraîche and then gradually beat in the icing sugar. Put the icing in the fridge for a little while so that it sets before you need to use it.

DRINKING WITH
CHOCOLATE

Micah Carr-Hill is our Product Development Manager and he is also a serious foodie. He became interested in wine when he worked in the wine shop, Oddbins, and eight years later, has poured most of his earnings into buying wine and cooking meals for his friends and his partner Nat that can take him days to prepare.

Micah believes that there should be no rules about what you should drink with particular foods, but says that 'chocolate and chocolate puddings are particularly difficult to match as they coat your mouth, are usually quite sweet and chocolate itself has a certain amount of acidity'. He therefore suggests a few tips:

'The one thing to bear in mind when matching wine to desserts is that it is best to choose a wine that is as sweet, if not sweeter, than the food otherwise the wine is likely to be overpowered by what you are eating and seem unpleasantly sharp.

'However, chocolate does not always go well with traditional sweet wines such as Sauternes and as chocolate is often married with cherries, raisins, dates and other such fruits, it often makes sense to match them with drinks that have similar flavours. For example, a chocolate pudding with raspberry would go well with a raspberry liqueur like Framboise or raspberry beer from Belgium.

'Lighter puddings made with white and milk chocolate work well with a fresh, spritzy, grapey Moscato d'Asti or a slightly heavier Orange Muscat (especially if they contain orange). Belgian cherry or raspberry beers would also be good.

'Puddings made with a dark chocolate demand a richer and fuller wine such as a Black Muscat or a sweet Italian Recioto, made from partially dried red wine grapes. You could also try a vin doux naturels, which is a type of French wine that is made from partially fermented wine and local brandy, such as Rivesaltes, Banyuls or Maury. A port, Ruby or Tawny, an Australian Liqueur Muscat, or even one of the sweeter Madeiras (Malmsey or Bual) would also be good choices.

'If you're serving a savoury dish such as a mole, you need a weighty red wine to cope with the range of rich flavours kicking about. A big Syrah, Shiraz or Zinfandel would cope as would a big Italian red such as an Amarone or Barolo.

'Stouts, porters and dark beers made from chocolate malts (that have been highly roasted) are also good companions as is black coffee, irrespective of whether there is coffee in the recipe or not.

'The following are my suggestions, but remember that there are no hard and fast rules:

COMPLEMENTARY FLAVOURS

APRICOT – light, sweet Muscat or a Hungarian Tokaji

APPLES – sweet Oloroso Sherry or a Liqueur Muscat

BANANA – Australian Liqueur Muscat, Tokaji, sweet Madeira or Tawny Port

BISCUITS – Tea, coffee, milk

BROWNIES – Black coffee or a good whisky

COFFEE – Coffee, Orange Muscat, Australian Liqueur Muscat or a sweet Oloroso sherry such as Matusalem

DATES – Liqueur Muscat or sweet Oloroso sherry

FIGS – Black Muscat or sweet Oloroso sherry

GINGER – Ginger beer, sweet Oloroso sherry or a Liqueur Muscat

GORGONZOLA   Sweet red Italian Recioto, late-bottled vintage Port or Tawny Port

HARE – a big Syrah, Shiraz or Zinfandel

HAZELNUTS – a Malmsey or Bual Madeira, or a stout made from chocolate malt

ICE CREAM – a Liqueur Muscat, sweet Oloroso or even a Pedro Ximinez (PX) sherry, a Malmsey or Bual Madeira

LAMB – a big red from the Rhone Valley, Portugal or southern Italy

LEMON – a very sweet late-harvest Riesling such as a Trockenbeerenauslese

MEXICAN – Chilean or Argentinian red wine, Mexican beer or a cocktail such as a Margarita or Bloody Mary

PANNA COTTA – Recioto di Soave from Italy or an Orange Muscat

PEARS – Orange Muscat

PECAN PIE – Liqueur Muscat, sweet Oloroso Muscat or a Malmsey or Bual Madeira

SAUSAGES – robust Spanish or Portuguese reds or a Zinfandel

STOUT CAKE – stout

TRUFFLES – eau de vie of your choice

VANILLA – late-harvest Riesling

VENISON – big Italian red such as a Barolo or something from the south such as a Salice Salentino

WALNUTS – Australian Liqueur Muscat or a sweet Oloroso sherry

WHITE CHOCOLATE – sweet white Bordeaux such as Sauternes or Barsac, or a late-harvest Riesling such as an Auslese or Beerenauslese.'

Lubaantun was the centre of the Maya civilisation in southern Belize. A great ceremonial focus, it existed over 1,000 years ago, hidden deep in the rainforest.

In this vibrant society, the universal measure of value was the cocoa bean. As Lubaantun was situated in the Maya mountains, where cacao trees thrived in the wild, it rapidly became the economic centre of the Maya world, with the cocoa bean at the heart of the economy.

In the 1850s, it was taken over by colonists, who logged the land and established plantations. But they struggled to control nature and place names like 'Go To Hell Creek' and 'Hellgate' are all that remains of those desperate times.

The Maya returned to their villages in the mountains and lived by subsistence farming, trading their surplus cocoa beans for cash and growing indigenous crops using traditional methods. But in the early 1990s the price of cocoa, which had been falling for years, dropped dramatically just before harvest time as too much cocoa flooded world markets and many farmers were left unable to afford even to harvest their crops.

It was at this time that Jo Fairley and Craig Sams, who were on holiday in Belize and looking for organic cocoa beans, heard about their plight. They began to buy organic beans from the Maya, which in turn, led to their involvement with the Fairtrade foundation. Their relationship with the Toledo Cocoa Growers Association resulted in the creation of Green & Black's

Maya Gold Chocolate, sold in the UK and the first-ever product to carry the Fairtrade Mark.

Over 300 families benefit from the sale of cocoa beans and many of the farmers have plantations with trees that are over 100 years old. They live on the land that their ancestors have farmed for thousands of years and will preserve that land for future generations.

Saul Garcia is a Fairtrade farmer who has been farming cacao in Belize for thirty-eight years. If you visit his fifteen-acre farm set on the banks of the Columbia river, you can see more than fifteen different varieties of cacao tree, surrounded by a cascade of beautiful colours from the shrubs and crops that he plants between his cacao trees.

The bio-diversity created by planting so many different species of cacao and other plants helps to reduce the threat of bugs that cause serious damage to organically grown cacao.

Papaya, bananas, coffee, breebee, coconut, mango, breadfruit, cacao, mamey sapote, lime, *Theobroma bicolor*, avocado, cohune palm, soursop, plantain, samwood, jippy japa, golden plum, leucaena, glyricidia, craboo, orange, starfruit, vanilla, ginger, sugar cane, sorrel and bamboo. These are just some of the plants Saul Garcia grows. Some are used for food or as fibre, particularly for basket weaving, others are good for the soil and there are also ornamental plants for attracting pollinators.

INDEX

ACKNOWLEDGEMENTS

Green & Black's and Caroline Jeremy would like to thank all the staff past and present at Green & Black's especially Micah Carr-Hill, Cluny Brown and Mark Palmer; all the farmers who grow cacao for us; Jo Fairley and Craig Sams our founders; all those people whose recipes have been included in this book; Christopher Nesbitt who has been the driving force behind the development of the TCGA in Belize, and his wife Dawn; Claire Fry who designed the book; Francesca Yorke for her photographs; David Morgan, the home economist; Wei Tang for her prop styling; the recipe testers Jo Gilks, Sally Leighton, Gilly Booth and Sofia Craxton; Kyle Cathie, Muna Reyal and Ana Sampson at Kyle Cathie our publishers; Pearlfisher, our packaging design company and Phipps PR.

We would also like to thank the following chefs, authors and publishers for giving us permission to use their recipes:

Alastair Little and Richard Whittington, Fudge Sauce, *Keep It Simple* (Conran Octopus 1993)
Tavola, 155 Westbourne Grove, London W11 2RS

Dodi Miller, Mole Poblano de Guajolote, Cool Chile Co. P.O. Box 5702, London W11 2GS

Elisabeth Luard, Italian Venison Agridolce, more recipes in *Latin American Kitchen* (Kyle Cathie 2002)

Elizabeth Weisberg and Rachel Duffield,
Lighthouse Bakery Chocolate Bread, Lighthouse Bakery, 64 Northcote Road, London SW11 6QL

Gerard Coleman and Anne Weyns, Chocolate Salted Caramel Tart,
L'Artisan du Chocolat, 89 Lower Sloane Street, London SW1 8DA

Gerhard Jenne, Chocolate Biscuit Cake, Konditor & Cook, 22 Cornwall Road, London SE1 8TW

The Groucho Club, Chocolate Eruptions, The Groucho Club, 45 Dean Street, London W1D 4QB

Launceston Place, Chocolate Berry Torte, Launceston Place 1a, Launceston Place, London W8

Lorna Wing, Sachertorte, Lorna Wing Ltd, 48 Westover Road, London SW18 2RH

Clementine Cake from *How to Eat* by Nigella Lawson, published by Chatto & Windus. Reprinted by permission of The Random House Group Ltd

Nora Carey, Chocolate and Chestnut Soufflés,
Perfect Preserves Provisions from the Kitchen Garden (Stewart, Tabori & Chang, 1990)

Paul and Jean Rankin, White Chocolate and Hazelnut Cheesecake, *Hot Chefs* (BBC Worldwide, 1992)
www.cayennerestaurant.com

Rachel Green, Chocolate and Lemongrass Mousse,
Rachel Green's Food Design, The Barn, St Leonard's Lane, South Cockerington, Louth, Lincolnshire LN11 7EF

Stuart Octzman, Fruit Cake, The Handmade Food Company,
18 Charleswood Road, Rashers Green Industrial Estate, Dereham NR19 1SX

Sue Lawrence, Chocolate Crusted Lemon Tart, *Book of Baking* (Headline 2004)

The New Covent Soup Company, Chocolate Soup,
The New Covent Garden Soup Company Book of Soups New, Old and Odd Recipes (Macmillan, London, UK 1996)

Valentina Harris, Tuscan Sweet and Sour Hare, *Regional Italian Cooking* (BBC Worldwide)
www.villavalentina.com (Cookery school in Tuscany).

White Chocolate Cardamom Mousse Reprinted by kind permission of Harper Collins Publishers Ltd.
© Nigel Slater, *Real Food* (1999)

Whole Earth Foods, Cocoa Crunch Kallo Foods, Wormley, Surrey GU8 5SZ

We also thank the following organisations:
The Fairtrade Foundation, Suite 204, 16 Baldwin's Gardens, London EC1N 7RJ Tel:020 7405 5942 www.fairtrade.org.uk
Soil Association, Bristol House, 40–56 Victoria Street, Bristol BS1 6BY Tel: 0117 929 0661 www.soilassociation.org
Toledo Cacao Growers Association, Punta Gorda Depot, Main Road, Punta Gorda, Toledo District, Belize.

Caroline would also like to thank her husband David and children Oscar, Edward, Chloë and Oliver for their tasting skills patience and enthusiasm for all things chocolate; Claire Fry, Jo Gilks, Gilly Booth, Beverley Patrick and Sally Johnston for endless creative thought, animated discussion and laughter.

First published in Great Britain 2003 by
Kyle Cathie Limited
23 Howland Street
London W1T 4AY
general.enquiries@kyle-cathie.com
www.kylecathie.com

15 17 19 20 18 16 14

ISBN 978 1 85626 700 7

Senior Editor Muna Reyal
Designer Claire Fry
Photographer Francesca Yorke
Home economist David Morgan
Copy editor Stephanie Horner
Recipe testing Jo Gilks, Sally Leighton, Gilly Booth
Styling Wei Tang
Production Sha Huxtable

A Cataloguing In Publication record for this title is available from the British Library.

Colour reproduction by Colourscan
Printed and bound in Singapore by Tien-Wah Press